DECOUPAGE ON

ON GLASS | WOOD | METAL | ROCKS | SHELLS
WAX | SOAP | PLASTIC | CANVAS | CERAMIC

Photographs by Jon Aron

CHILTON BOOK COMPANY
Radnor, Pennsylvania

DECOUPAGE ON GLASS WOOD METAL ROCKS SHELLS WAX SOAP PLASTIC CANVAS CERAMIC

Leslie Linsley

Library of Congress Cataloging in Publication Data

Linsley, Leslie.
    Decoupage on . . . glass, wood, metal, rocks, shells,
wax, soap, plastic, canvas, ceramic.

    (Creative crafts series)
    1. Decoupage.   I. Title.
TT870.L5416   745.54   77-3527
ISBN 0-8019-6497-0
ISBN 0-8019-6498-9 pbk.

1 2 3 4 5 6 7 8 9 0   5 4 3 2 1 0 9 8 7

For my grandfather, Emil Zuckerman,
and my mother, Ruth Linsley,
two crafty people

Contents

List of Illustrations

List of Color Illustrations

1
Introduction

DECOUPAGE ON

Another decoupage book? Why? That's the question I had to ask myself when I sat down to write this book. It seems as though I've been doing decoupage all my life. A few years ago I didn't think that I could create ideas that I hadn't already done. During that time, however, I began to experiment with some things that I hadn't tried before. Also during that time there were new developments in the craft business. New products came onto the market. Decoupage became more popular than it had ever been before. All kinds of designs appeared in the form of wrapping paper, greeting cards, posters and unusual picture books and even transfer designs requiring no cutting. And just when I thought I would never do another decoupage project, I would get turned on to a new idea. So I guess that decoupage will always be a part of my life no matter what else I am involved with.

But then I was faced with the problem of what would make this book different from the others that I have written. The answer seemed quite obvious. Since decoupage has always been taught pretty much the way it was done years and years ago, most hobbyists thought of it as a longtime commitment. In other words, one started a decoupage project and knew that it was something that would involve a certain amount of time to complete. This time usually meant a minimum of a week, and most times much longer. The projects would therefore have to justify the time spent and if one didn't turn out the way you expected, it was a real let down.

Then of course there were those people who were mildly curious about this craft, but felt that it was too complicated to learn. Many busy people simply didn't want to spend that much time on a craft project no matter how great the results. Not everyone wants to become an expert in the art of decoupage even though he or she might want to try a simple project.

The craft and hobby manufacturers have recognized this fact and have been doing something to solve this problem. They have since developed quick and easy materials to eliminate the hours that it used to take. There is now fast-drying varnish and a project can be completed in less than a half hour. The wrapping papers so readily available in stationery stores are sensational. And best of all the plaques, boxes, containers and other objects on which to do decoupage are available everywhere. All these things combined add up to a very exciting prospect, one that I couldn't ignore.

After all my years of doing time-consuming decoupage, actually enjoying the fact that it was taking so long to complete a project, I am intrigued with the prospect of instant decoupage. So before beginning this book, I collected many interesting designs and ideas that could be done in less than a day. Some of the projects have been done before, but I have tried to create new and interesting ways to approach them. Some were done using found objects; some with new products strictly found in craft shops. Of course, I couldn't ignore a few projects that held to the old tradition. But these are not difficult and have a contemporary feeling. All of them were fun, easy and a little unusual. I used every kind of surface that I could think of that might work. Thus the title: *Decoupage On*, which for me also means that decoupage can go on and on and on.

DECOUPAGE IS

Decoupage is the eighteenth century craft that the French are most commonly credited with originating. However, it has been practiced in almost every country in the world. Quite literally it is a French word that means "applied cutouts." A *coupier* is a cutter. The craft of decoupage requires some paint, a pair of scissors, a print, some glue and a surface for applying the print. The technique is relatively uncomplicated. Decoupage is an ideal craft for creative expression. Even the beginner need not be slowed down by a long period of becoming adept at difficult procedures.

Practically every contemporary artist has used the decoupage technique. Picasso, who seems to have originated everything in modern art, together with Braque, got the Cubist movement going. Their first works were done with cut paper elements. But the outstanding user of cut paper has to be Matisse. He did many works, including a delightful book called *Jazz*, made of decoupage designs. In his later years, he was confined to bed and worked almost exclusively with cut paper. His masterpiece, the chapel in Vence, was designed in its entirety with decoupage.

Decoupage has been applied to everything from furniture to the tiniest thimble (Fig. 1–1). In the earliest days of decoupage, when the craft was done in its purest form, very ornate pieces of furniture were completely covered with the most elaborate handcolored cutout designs. In England, Victorian ladies spent

Fig. 1–1 A small wooden trinket box designed by Amy Brunhuber.

much leisure time coloring and cutting out designs for decoupage. Most of these early projects took months to complete. In those days before color printing there was also no varnish. Lacquer was applied over the piece many times until the surface was as smooth as glass.

Today decoupage is no longer an art form available only to those who can afford to hire an artist to decorate their home. It has become a popular craft that anyone can do. It is simple to learn, requires little space, is inexpensive and the materials are readily available. No longer confined to furniture pieces, the most popular items seem to be wooden boxes and plaques. And with the modern materials that manufacturers are constantly bringing out, a decoupage project can be completed in a day. As if all this weren't enough to make for the perfect craft, there is an endless potential for creative expression using this technique.

Decoupage can be applied to wood, metal, glass, plastic, clay, ceramic, wax, shells, rocks, canvas, paper, soap and even fingernails. Most often done on wood, the surface is first sanded smooth and then painted (Fig. 1–2). Once the paint dries, the surface is again sanded lightly to smooth out any imperfections or brush strokes. Next the design is cut out. Books, wrapping paper, greeting cards, photographs, wallpaper or prints made especially for decoupage are excellent sources for decoupage designs. Almost any subject can be found in printed materials; if it can be cut out, it can be used for decoupage.

Once the design is cut out, it is glued to the surface of the object you are working on. Several coats of varnish are then applied right over the design so that the entire object is covered. Each coat of varnish is sanded smooth before the

Fig. 1–2 Wooden plaques can also be used as coasters. Designed by Ruth Linsley.

next coat is applied. Once the project has several coats of varnish and has been sanded so that it is smooth to the touch, it can be antiqued or simply waxed to protect it. When making a box, you might like to line it with wrapping paper or wallpaper or fabric. And that's all there is to the process. The creative part is up to you. This is what will make your project uniquely yours. And of course that's the part that makes people enjoy this craft so much.

Once the technique is learned, you will begin to think of ideas for creating new and exciting projects using a wide variety of designs that you might find. Decoupage is a great way to make personal gifts, to raise money for local functions, to give a new look to worn out objects in your home and, best of all, for personal creative enjoyment.

2
Materials and How to Use Them

PAINT

If you will be working on a small object such as a plaque or a box, rather than a piece of furniture, it must first be painted. Acrylic paint is best for this (Fig. 2–1). This is a water-base paint which dries quickly, covers well in one or two coats and comes in absolutely every color imaginable. Usually found in art supply or craft shops, it comes in tubes as well as small jars. This paint can be thinned with water and, when the painting is finished, your brush can be cleaned easily in warm soap and water. These colors can be mixed to make other colors. You will soon be looking for more things to paint simply because the colors are so much fun to create. This paint covers well and is quite thick; therefore you need very little. Simply squeeze a small amount on a piece of cardboard, for instance, and mix your other color right over it. Or you can use the color as it comes from the tube. If you are buying a bright color, it is a good idea to also purchase a tube of white. Often the colors are quite intense and need softening by adding a little white for lightener. Several manufacturers such as Grumbacher, Palmer, Weber or Liquitex make acrylic paint.

Indoor house paint such as latex is also fine for decoupage. The flat water-base paint is best, covers easily and dries in minutes. If you have some in the house, you might save some time and money by using it for any wood projects that won't be used outdoors. The latex paint is not as thick as the acrylic, but it does sand to a smoother finish because it is less rubbery. Because this is a water-base paint, you can rinse your brush out in water when you have finished painting. The pastel colors usually require at least two, often three, coats of paint in order to completely cover the object so that the wood doesn't show through. The darker colors often cover in just one coat.

5

Fig. 2–1 Acrylic paint is best
for most decoupage projects.

Enamel or oil-base paint is often used for pieces of furniture or on outdoor projects. This paint takes twenty-four hours to dry. It is a good idea to apply a sealer coat to your object before painting it. A sealer is a primer that you buy in the hardware or craft shop. It seals the pores so that your first coat of paint will not seep into the wood. It provides a smooth finish on which to apply your paint; thus a smoother, more professional looking paint job. The enamel paint comes in a flat finish, semigloss and glossy. The flat enamel is mostly used for decoupage. Since this paint has an oil base, you will also need a brush cleaner for soaking your brush when you are through and for cleaning your hands and any spatters around your work area. I do not recommend oil-base paint if you can avoid it. Outdoor furniture, mail boxes or a boat would require outdoor paint which is more economical when purchased in large quantity from a hardware store.

When painting a small object, you should use an appropriate size brush (Fig. 2–2). Apply the paint to the entire piece. If you paint all your strokes in one direction, your piece will look best. Be sure to cover all areas. If you are working on a box with hinges, they do not have to be removed in order to paint. This is not necessary, nor is it practical. Simply paint around the hinges very carefully. If you get a little paint on them, wipe it away with a rag. If some paint dries on the hinges, it can be scraped away with a razor blade. Or you can leave it. If you plan to antique your box, the antiquing will cover the area on your hinge that has been accidentally painted. It is far easier to carefully paint around hinges than to remove them and replace them after you have painted. Even if you intend to line your box when you have finished, don't forget to paint the inside rim. Once the box has been painted, be sure to prop it open slightly so that it will not stick shut.

If you are painting a plaque, try to paint all your strokes in one direction, avoiding excess brush marks. If you are working on a piece of furniture, you will have to be especially careful when painting since the object is so large. Because of the size, the painting becomes more obvious if it hasn't been done well. A good paint job gives you a base for a most professional looking decoupage piece. If the painting is sloppy, it will show through the varnish and there will be nothing you can do to correct this. So don't rush the painting. It doesn't really take that long to do it well.

If your piece needs more than one coat, let the first coat of paint dry thoroughly, then sand it slightly before applying another coat. This sanding will remove any imperfections that have dried in the paint. There are often tiny paint particles that give the surface of your object a bumpy look when dry. Or, when using acrylic paint, the brush strokes are often apparent when dry. These can be smoothed out when sanding. Just do the sanding lightly before applying another coat of paint. Check the sanding section for correct grade of sandpaper and how to use it. If you are not planning to line your box, you might consider painting

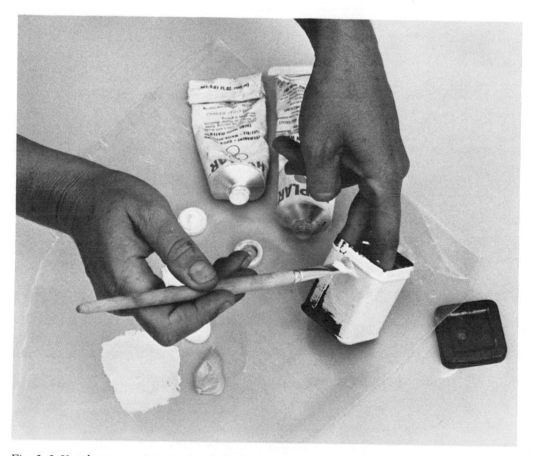

Fig. 2–2 Use the appropriate size brush for the item you are working on.

the inside with a contrasting color. It is interesting to have, for instance, a light pastel color on the outside and a contrasting darker shade on the inside. You could then save one of your cutouts to apply to the inside for added interest.

Acrylic and oil paint work best on metal although there are specially made paints for metal, such as Rust-oleum. This is not necessary for a small project and I would recommend using the acrylic or latex paint because it dries quickly and is easier to use. However, you must handle the object carefully because the paint is likely to chip or peel before it is covered with varnish. In other words, when you are finished painting it, the object should be put aside to dry. When you are applying your cutout designs to a painted metal object, be careful not to drop or bang it so that you will not have to touch up spots where the paint has come off. Once the varnish has been applied, the piece will be protected from damage.

If you are painting an outdoor object, be sure to cover all sides including the bottom. If the entire piece is not sealed with paint, and then varnish, moisture can get into it. If this happens, you run the risk of the entire finish peeling away. When painting a metal tray, it is a good idea to paint the bottom as well as the top. Once you have applied your varnish to the top, a coat should also be applied to the bottom.

STAIN

Wood stain comes in many different finishes. This is an excellent base for unfinished pieces of furniture. Hardware stores usually stock different wood stains and have sample colors on display. These have an oil base so you will need a brush cleaner for cleaning your brush after applying the stain. This is quite simple to apply. Often it doesn't even require a brush; some people prefer to use a rag and wipe it over the area. The stain sinks into the wood, penetrating the surface and immediately changing the color. You rub it over the entire surface, wait a few minutes and then wipe away the excess. After that allow it to dry overnight. Often a second coat is desirable to make the piece darker. However, since you will be applying several coats of varnish once the piece is decoupaged, this will make the color darker and richer.

A small can of stain covers quite a bit of surface. It is used directly from the can and only needs a little stirring before applying. If you are making a plaque for a den or an office, you might consider using stain rather than paint. If the wood grain of your piece is especially nice, it is a shame to cover it with paint. In this case it would be much better to apply a wood stain. Rather than cover, the stain brings out and emphasizes the natural grain of the wood. Often it will look brighter and more interesting than if left in its natural state. When applying stain to a large object, do this in a well-ventilated room. If the weather is nice, this project can be done outdoors.

SANDPAPER

Sanding is an essential part of the decoupage process. Almost all surfaces must be prepared for decoupage by sanding first. If you are working on a wood surface, almost anything that you buy will need to be sanded. Even when the wood appears to be pretty smooth, there may be dust particles that should have a once-over with the sandpaper. This does not have to be done with a heavy hand. As a matter of fact, it should be done very lightly and then the grit from the sanding is dusted off the piece before applying paint or stain.

The best kind of sandpaper for decoupage is a black wet-or-dry flint paper. This can be purchased in most hobby and craft stores as well as hardware stores. The 3M WetorDry paper is best for all your decoupage work. Buy the finest grade you can get, #600, unless you are refinishing a piece. If you have purchased an old box with a finish already on it, you will need a medium #320 grade sandpaper to go over the piece. This sanding will remove any wax that might be covering the piece. It is not necessary to completely remove the old finish before painting. A thorough sanding job will do the trick. If your piece is metal, it doesn't hurt to give it a quick once-over with a fine #400 sandpaper so that the paint will sink into the surface better.

Once the first coat of paint has dried, you will lightly sand the entire piece with the fine #400 sandpaper. Do not wet it. Use it dry for this first sanding. After you have applied the designs and the varnish, you will sand each coat of varnish lightly with #600 before applying another coat. This should be done with a very light touch so that you will not sand away the designs. I suggest that you wet the sandpaper slightly for this. Each time your varnish coat dries, you will sand it before going on. If the sandpaper is slightly damp, it will make the varnished surface smoother. For your last sanding of the final step, dip the piece of #600 sandpaper into a cup of warm soapy water. Rub this over your surface for an extra smooth finish (Fig. 2–3). Wipe away all excess dirt and sand grit after this.

Fig. 2–3 For final sanding use #600 sandpaper.

BRUSHES

Before purchasing your decoupage brushes, you really must decide what the project is going to be. This will determine the size of your brush. Usually a half-inch or one-inch brush is good for most projects. If you are working on a piece of furniture, you might like to purchase a much wider brush. The best decoupage brush is a flat, natural hair varnish brush. This is available in art supply, hobby and craft shops and needn't be expensive. Often new brushes shed hairs when you first use them. Simply wet your brush and pull the ends so that you remove the loose ones. In this way you will not have to be picking them out of your newly painted surface. If some do come off on your paint, use a razor blade or the tip of your scissors to remove them. If they dry on the surface, use the razor blade to scrape them off. It is not difficult. A loose dried hair can often be sanded away when you are going over the surface.

A natural hair brush, when kept clean, is the surest guarantee of a fine varnish finish. After each use, your brush should be carefully cleaned and put away. If you will be using an oil-base paint or varnish, after cleaning the brush, wrap it in plastic wrap, such as Saran Wrap or Handi-Wrap to keep it soft for later use.

Another kind of brush that is excellent for the quick little projects that we will be doing is a polyfoam brush. This brush looks like a piece of foam rubber on a stick. It is an inexpensive brush and is perfect for painting or varnishing with water-base varnish. It is usually referred to as a throw-away brush because it is only used for one or two projects. After that it becomes stiff and not much good for decoupage. You will have fewer brush strokes using this brush and it is the only thing to use for decoupage under glass.

If you will be using a water-base paint and then an oil base varnish, it is best to buy two different brushes. It is unwise to use the same brush for both. Your varnish brush should really remain in the brush cleaner between coats of varnish. Once your painting is complete, the brush should be cleaned and put away for another time.

VARNISH

While indoor wood varnish has always been used for decoupage, the projects shown here were done mostly with a water-base, fast-drying varnish. There are several kinds of varnish, each used for a different purpose. The oil-base varnishes take twenty-four hours to dry and produce the best results in terms of a smooth, hard, long-lasting finish. Most indoor wood varnishes can also be used for metal surfaces and come in a glossy or matte finish. The matte is a satiny finish while the glossy creates a glass-like surface.

The varnish that you use is simply a matter of preference. Hobby and craft shops also carry the water-base varnish which is quick drying and often five coats can be applied within a half hour. The finish is tough, but cannot be sanded as smooth as the other. It is an excellent product for quick projects. This varnish is called polymer medium and also comes in a matte or shiny finish. Some of the brand names are Grumbacher, Liquitex, Palmer or Weber. This varnish can be cleaned up with water, and warm soapy water will clean your brush in an instant. It cannot, however, be used for outdoor projects such as a mailbox. The change in temperature causes it to turn murky white in color and it will crack and peel off. There are varnishes made especially for outdoor use and they will say this on the label.

If you are not sure about a product, read the label. This is important when doing decoupage as some materials do not mix well with others.

To apply any kind of varnish, it is best if it's not too thick. Do not put so much on at once that the varnish drips. If you brush the varnish in one direction and then back the other way, it will be fine. Then just put the object on an out-of-the-way shelf to dry. If you are using the water varnish, it will dry in minutes. You can then sand it and apply another coat. It will take about five minutes for each coat and you can cover most projects with five coats.

If you have applied the oil-base varnish, you will have to use a brush cleaner, such as turpentine or mineral spirits to clean your brush between coats. Do not sand the varnished surface until your project is completely dry. This will take twenty-four hours.

Polyurethane is another kind of varnish finish that is used primarily for outdoor projects and furniture. It gives a hard, almost plastic-like finish and is applied just like your oil-base varnish. It is more expensive than varnish and has a strong odor.

DESIGNS

Decoupage designs that used to take hours to cut out can now be found in simplified versions. For instance, there are a variety of rub-on transfers for projects that can be done quickly and with quite good results. The designs are made by Letraset in England and Heirloom Crafts in the United States. These designs, while limited in scope, are easily applied. They are similar to a decal, but no water is required and you simply rub them onto the surface of your project. Then, varnish over them and the design is permanent.

Other sources of contemporary and easily obtained cutouts are stationery stores. The greeting paper and cards available today are varied and exciting. I used this source almost exclusively for the projects in this book. Postcards and photographs are used as well as invitations, books, pre-stick seals and real flowers (Fig. 2–4).

Strictly speaking, decoupage means cutting out and unless a design is created by cutting it from paper it is not considered decoupage. However, since the focus of this book is quick and easy projects, almost anything goes and we will stretch the point whenever possible.

Valentines, doilies and even ribbons can be used effectively. Wallpaper can be used for lining boxes. Magazines, while most times too thin, can occasionally work. Most craft shops carry designs made just for decoupage and this is a good place to find lining papers as well. The only material that was not used is cut-out

Fig. 2–4 Design ideas can come from many sources. Pressed flowers are used on this plant holder.

fabric. It is excellent for lining boxes but not for the actual designs (Fig. 2–5). The material frays when cut and it cannot be varnished successfully. Almost any subject can be found in printed material and if it can be cut out, it can be used for decoupage.

SCISSORS

Cuticle scissors are most commonly used for decoupage cutting. The curved pointed shape is excellent for cutting in and out of all fine points. Embroidery scissors are good to use when you have a large print or poster to cut apart. Larger scissors are used to cut wallpaper or wrapping paper for lining boxes.

When cutting out your designs, try to cut away as much of the excess background paper as possible. A fine cutting job will show up well against your painted or stained background (Fig. 2–6). If a print is too large to fit onto your object, simply cut it apart so that it will fit well. If something is too small but you would really like to use it, find something that you can add to fill in the overall design. For very intricate cutting, take your time and cut the hardest to get at places first. When choosing a design, select one that you know you will be able to cut, rather than one that simply looks pretty.

Fig. 2–5 Decoupage purse by Ruth Linsley.

Fig. 2–6 The lining for this box is made from a delicate lace handkerchief. Designed by Ruth Linsley.

GLUE

Once your designs have been cut out, they are applied with glue. Use a white glue such as Sobo or Elmer's Glue-All. Squirt a small amount of glue onto the back of your design. Using your fingers, spread the glue from the middle to all sides, making sure that the edges have enough glue on them. Place the paper piece down on the surface of your project. With the palm of your hand, press it firmly in place. Using a damp sponge, pat the design while wiping away the excess glue that may escape from the edges. You may want to roll the brush handle over the design, in order to be sure that it is very secure.

If your design is placed so that it goes from bottom to top, such as in the front of the box, you will cut it apart once it is glued in place. This is done with a razor blade just at the opening where the top and bottom of the box come together. If you place some designs on the side and you want them to spread across the opening, cut them the same way. Wait until all the designs have been glued in place and then cut apart where needed.

If you are working on a large piece, such as furniture, you might use a rolling pin or a brayer to smooth out designs, thus eliminating air bubbles.

WAX

When the decoupage projects are finished, many crafters apply a coat of furniture paste wax to protect the finish. This wax is clear and is applied to boxes, plaques, furniture, metal projects and even plastic. The different brands are: Butcher's, Johnson's and Goddard, to name a few. They are available in the supermarket or hardware stores. A thin coat is rubbed over the surface with a clean rag. The wax is left to dry for ten minutes. Then, using a soft cloth, rub and buff until the surface glows. If this is done every six months, your project will be well taken care of.

3

Decoupage On Wood

Wood is the best and most traditional surface for applying the decoupage technique. Some of the projects that can be done are wall plaques, boxes of every conceivable size and shape, furniture, candlesticks, napkin rings, planters, tissue holders, picture frames, lightswitch plates, salt and pepper shakers and even a door (Fig. 3–1). Most boxes, plaques and similar containers mentioned are available in craft and hobby shops. Sometimes an unusual item can be found in an antique or junk shop. Often an item that is marred or chipped and isn't too appealing can be salvaged, even made beautiful, through the decoupage process.

Most of the wooden items found in craft shops are made of white pine or birch wood. They are fairly smooth to begin with, requiring little sanding to prepare the surface for painting or staining. Redwood objects are excellent for outdoor projects because this wood will not warp, rot or change its shape due to changes in the weather.

If the object that you uncover in a junk shop is in poor condition and the wood is not particularly pretty, don't give it a second thought. Since the process of decoupage requires a couple of coats of paint and several coats of varnish, the original finish will be completely covered. If you do find something that already has a finish, it can be easily sanded and painted over. If you are working on a large piece of furniture, the original finish can be removed with a paint remover. If the piece has a shellacked finish, it can be removed with wood alcohol that is sold in a hardware store. Unfinished furniture lends itself beautifully to decoupage designs. Posters can be cut up to accommodate the large area that will be covered. When purchasing paint or stain for wooden objects, be sure to buy the right quantity. Choosing the right size brush is important as well.

If you have found an item or have an old piece of furniture that is made of a

Fig. 3–1 Handcolored prints for this box by Ruth Linsley.

particularly pretty wood, you can decoupage right on the bare wood. This might be more interesting than painting it. Most wooden objects sold in craft shops, however, are made of inferior woods since they are intended for the decoupage process which will cover the surface.

SEWING BOX

Materials Needed

small wooden box
greeting card
piece of wallpaper for lining
paint
brush for painting and varnishing
sponge
varnish (either oil base or water)
cuticle scissors

razor blade
glue (water-base varnish can be used as glue)
small piece of cardboard
cotton batting
piece of felt or other material
sandpaper #400 and #600

Directions

The box used for this sewing box is approximately 5″ x 4″ and 2″ high. This one is hinged and has a catch on the front which is optional and can be purchased in a craft shop (Fig. 3–2). Using white acrylic paint this box was given two coats of paint (Fig. 3–3). Each coat should dry for approximately twenty minutes before sanding. Once the paint is dry it should be lightly sanded with #400 sandpaper to create a smooth surface on which to apply the designs. The inside

Fig. 3–2 Handmade box is used for sewing supplies.

rim is painted with a rose color paint created by combining white with a cadmium red. The colors you choose should correspond to the design that you will use. It is a good idea to choose the design and the box at the same time before selecting your paint color. In this way you will be sure that the design will fit the object. If you do not intend to line the inside of the box, you should paint the entire inside rather than just the rim.

If you are using a greeting card, you might find that the paper is quite thick. You can thin the design by peeling away a layer of paper from the back of the

Fig. 3–3 Paint carefully around hinges and catches. Do not remove them first.

card. Using your cuticle scissors lift a corner of one edge. Carefully pull away the paper so that the entire back layer is removed. This will make it easier to cut out the design and once glued in place will require fewer coats of varnish to submerge it.

Cut out the entire design that you will use (Fig. 3–4). If more is needed,

Fig. 3–4 A greeting card is perfect for the sewing box design.

select added material from wrapping paper or a book. The flowers that were added to the front and sides of this box were cut from wrapping paper used for another project. The colors match the overall main design. The thread was a bit too fine to cut. In this case that part of the design was drawn on separately, using a fine sable artist's brush and a matching acrylic paint (Fig. 3–5). The paint was mixed to be the same color as the spool of thread.

Spread the glue to all edges of each cutout and lay in place. You should first determine where each piece will go before actually gluing it down. Once the design is glued to the surface, it is almost impossible to remove it. Have a damp sponge next to you when doing this. Use it to press each piece down and for wiping away excess glue around the edges of each cutout.

The flowers can be glued in such a way as to span the opening of the box. All the pieces are glued onto the box before cutting them apart. Once the flowers are dry a razor blade is used to make the slit separating the design so that the box can be opened. Wait for the design to dry (about five minutes) before cutting, then varnish (Fig. 3–6). If the cutout is wet, it will tear when cutting through it.

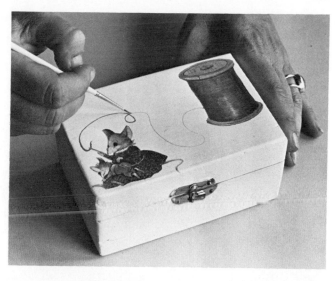

Fig. 3–5 The thread is too delicate to cut out. Paint this with
an artist's brush.

Fig. 3–6 The varnish protects
the design and surface of the
box.

   The lining used for this box is a small piece of wallpaper made for doll-
houses. This miniature wallpaper is available in craft shops. If you can't find this
you can use regular wallpaper or wrapping paper. Contact paper with self-
adhesive backing works well. Be sure to choose a paper with a small overall pattern. The area to cover is quite small and a large pattern will be too overpowering.

   The color and pattern that is used should correspond to the overall outside
design. When selecting the lining, hold it up to the outside to see if it will clash.

The design used here is small rose-colored flowers on a beige background. The rose-colored inside rim picks up the color from the lining.

Measure all walls, top and bottom of the inside of the box. Cut out pieces that are slightly bigger than the measurements (Fig. 3–7). Each piece should overlap on the bottom and sides just slightly (Fig. 3–8). In this way the corners

Fig. 3–7 A delicate wallpaper design is excellent for the lining.

Fig. 3–8 The lining pieces should overlap a tiny bit on the sides and bottom.

will all be covered. When the glue is applied to the paper, it will become wet. As the paper dries it shrinks a little bit. This is why it is a good idea to make the pieces a tiny bit larger than the actual measure. Glue each piece in place just as you did the design cutouts. You can cut one large piece that will extend from the back wall, down and across the bottom of the inside and up the inside front wall. First glue both of the sides in place, then glue this larger piece. Excess lining can be trimmed neatly with a single-edged razor blade (Fig. 3–9). The rim can then be painted in a contrasting color (Fig. 3–10).

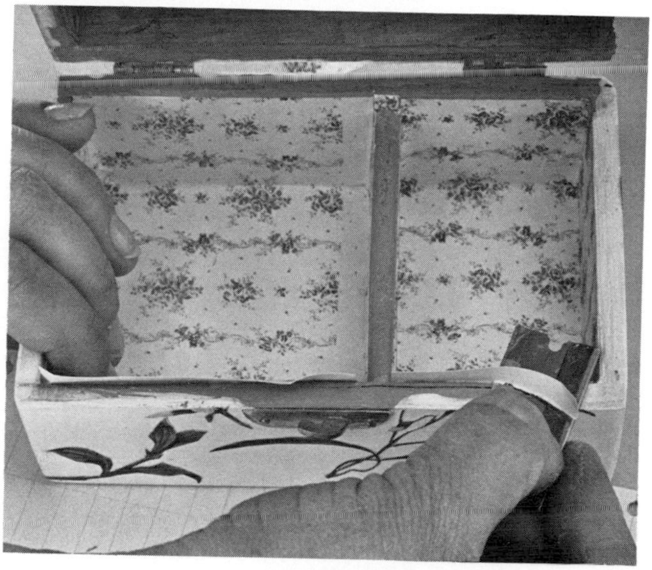

Fig. 3–9 Trim any excess lining with a razor blade.

Fig. 3–10 Repaint the rim in a contrasting color.

You can line the top the same way as the bottom unless you would like to make a pincushion in the top lid. First line all the sides with the paper. This pincushion is made from dark green corduroy fabric which goes well with the paper colors (Fig. 3–11). Then measure the inside lid. Using a piece of cardboard, such

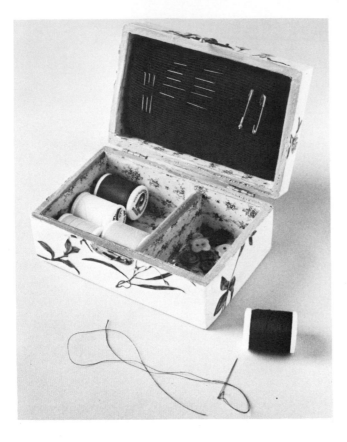

Fig. 3–11 A padded cushion set into the lid makes a built-in pincushion.

as shirt board, cut out a square that is just about one-eighth inch smaller on all sides (Fig. 3–12). This will give you room to wrap the fabric over the cardboard. Any kind of padding can be used for the cushion. Cut two or three pieces of cotton batting the same size as the cardboard. Place the layers of padding on top of the cardboard (Fig. 3–13). A drop of glue between each layer will hold them in place for easy handling. Cut a piece of material so that it is a half inch larger than the cardboard on all sides. This material can be felt, corduroy, velvet or similarly heavy fabric.

Apply glue to the back of the cardboard piece and lay it face down in the center of the material so that the glued side is on top (Fig. 3–14). Cut the corners off the material. Fold each side of the material up and over onto the glued cardboard. Apply more glue around the edge, covering the material that has been folded under. Turn the whole thing over and lay it into the lid. Keep your hands clean so that you don't get glue on the front of the material. Use a butter knife to press the edges into place. This will dry quickly, securing the pincushion to the inside lid.

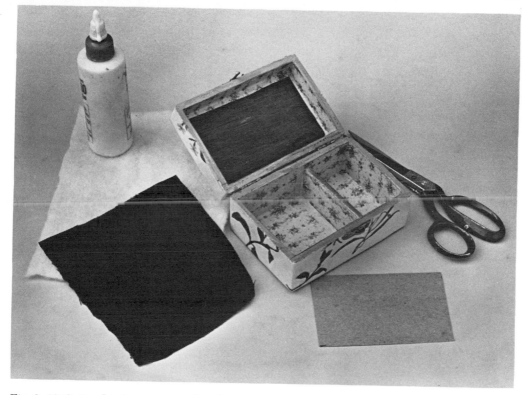

Fig. 3–12 Cotton batting, a piece of corduroy and cardboard are used to make the pincushion.

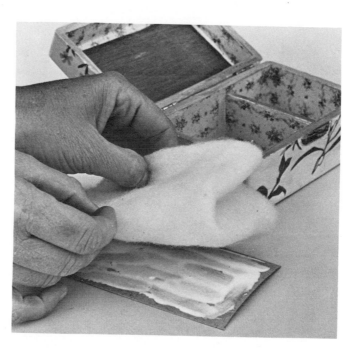

Fig. 3–13 Double the padding and glue it to the cardboard.

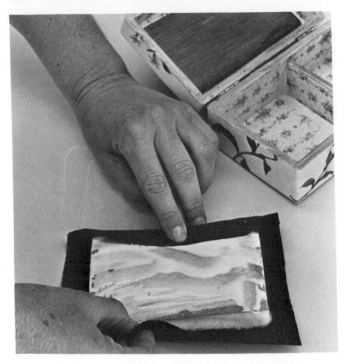

Fig. 3–14 Wrap the fabric around the padding and secure onto the cardboard backing.

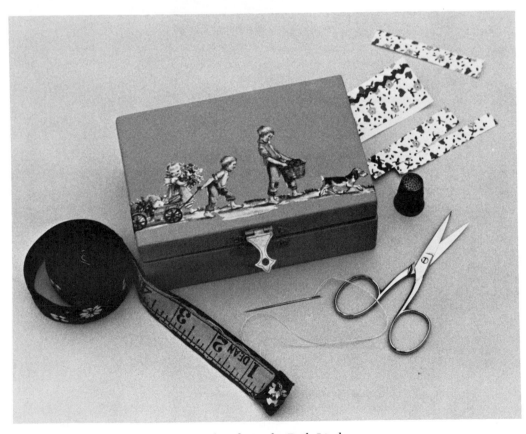

Fig. 3–15 Another version of a sewing box design by Ruth Linsley.

Using either a water-base varnish or indoor wood varnish, coat the entire outside of the box. Apply varnish to the bottom inside, over the paper lining and including the rim. Prop the box open so that the inside has air circulating around it. If you have used a long-drying varnish, put the box out of the way for twenty-four hours. After this time you will sand the outside only and the inside rim using the wet-or-dry sandpaper #600. If you have used the polymer medium (water varnish), apply coat after coat as each dries. In this way you will be able to finish this project in less than a day. Apply at least five coats of the varnish of your choice. The oil-base indoor varnish will give the box a smoother finish; but the fast-drying varnish, when applied carefully, has a strong finish also. This box has a matte rather than glossy finish.

Sand the final coat of varnish and apply a thin coat of paste wax to preserve the finish. You might want to line the entire box with fabric. This is done the same way as the pincushion, eliminating the padding. Simply cut out a piece of cardboard for each side and bottom and wrap the fabric around it before gluing in place. Try each piece before applying the glue to be sure that it will fit properly. A piece of the wallpaper can be applied to the bottom of the box (Fig. 3–16). A piece of felt can be used instead of the wallpaper for a finishing touch (Fig. 3–15).

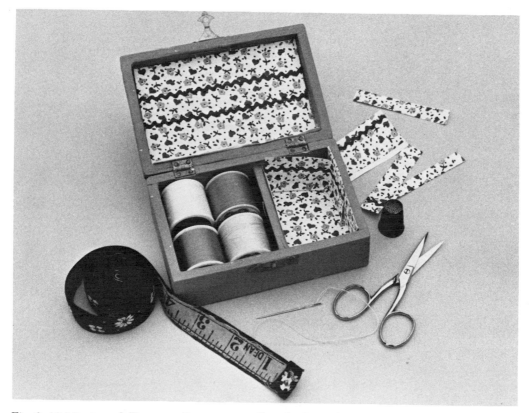

Fig. 3–16 Minature dollhouse wallpaper is excellent for lining boxes. Measure and cut the pieces before gluing in place.

OUTDOOR PLANTER

Materials Needed

redwood planter (this one is 11″ square
   and 12″ high)
book of wildflowers (or several similar
   prints)
white glue
cuticle scissors

polyurethane or outdoor varnish
paint (2 colors)
paintbrush
sandpaper #220 and #400 or #600
brush cleaner (mineral spirits or
   turpentine)

Directions

Planters are available at garden shops, discount department stores as well as craft shops. They come in all sizes and shapes and make wonderful decoupage projects (see Fig. 3–18). They are made primarily of redwood which is an excellent material for this project as it will not warp or rot. Many people who do decoupage are put off by redwood because of the color. It is true that if you are using a background color that is pastel or white you must apply two or three coats of paint in order to cover it. However, once covered, the red color cannot be seen. There are many planters made of a softer wood, such as pine or a white wood that can be found in the craft stores. Often a wastebasket made of wood can substitute for a planter.

Before beginning this project look around for designs that appeal to you. Since there are four sides to cover, the cutouts should relate and come from the same source. In this way they will match in color and style. There are many inexpensive paperback books available which are an excellent source for designs that are of one subject. For example, The Golden Book series has a book of wildflowers, one of birds, another of butterflies, shells, animals, insects and many others. If you can find similar prints that seem to look well together that is fine. Be sure not to buy prints that are too small for the item you are working on. If you have chosen a hexagonal or octagonal planter be sure to buy enough prints to cover all sides so that each side is related to the others. Choose designs that relate in color as well as style. Designing this object will take the most amount of time and is well worth the care taken. Since it is a large surface that you will be working on, the design must be planned carefully.

This item should be sanded until smooth. Redwood is quite porous and not as smooth as some of the white woods. Begin by sanding all exposed areas, including the inside and bottom, with the #220 sandpaper. This does not have to be done with a very heavy hand. Smooth over the surface so that the paint will go on evenly. If you use a sealer or primer coat of paint before beginning, this will coat the planter thus making the sanding and painting easier (Fig. 3–17). The sealer or primer is available in a paint or hardware store as well as some craft shops. Be prepared with enough paint to apply three coats of paint to the item if necessary. You can use an acrylic paint or enamel. The enamel will protect the object best from weather changes that can distort the shape. However, if you will keep the planter indoors much of the time you can use a water-base paint which will make the job easier for you. Don't forget to paint the bottom. This will seal the wood so that moisture cannot get under the finish.

Fig. 3–17 A redwood planter is a good outdoor decoupage project.

Choose a color paint that will be a pleasing background for your designs. This planter is painted sky blue so that the flowers look as though they are growing against the sky. Most wildflowers are yellow, orange, white or pale pastel colors and the blue of the sky is a good color complement for this design. The acrylic colors are quite vibrant; therefore in order to mix a sky blue or other pale background color use primarily white. Just a drop of the color is added to the white and then mixed. More color can be added as needed. Mix enough at one time to cover the entire object. Beige or off-white is another good background color that seems to look well with any color combination the flowers might be. The inside is painted moss green for contrast. The rim is painted with the moss green also. This picks up the green of the stems and leaves on the flowers.

When painting, brush in one direction only. This will help you to achieve a smoothly painted surface and will require little sanding. Sand each coat of paint once it is completely dry. Use the #400 or #600 sandpaper for this. The painted surface should be smooth and free of brush strokes and particles before applying the cutouts.

The cutting for this project is quite time consuming, unless you have chosen four large pictures to use. However, if you will be using a flower motif, you will be spending some time cutting. Use your cuticle scissors and cut the most difficult parts of the flowers first. Be sure to cut away all excess white paper so that it will not show up against the colored background. A neat cutting job is important when cutting such delicate pieces. This is a project to do after you have tried

some of the other easier ones. If you have selected a design that is too difficult to
cut, put it aside to use for something else. You will need quite a few flowers to
cover this object. Some can be larger than others. In this way you can spend time
cutting the more delicate designs without getting bogged down with the cutting.
If you have areas that look sparse, find grass blades that you can cut out to fill in
with. These are easy to cut out, but are in keeping with the delicate flower
designs. Avoid using prints that are heavy alongside those that are light and lacy.
This will create an unbalanced looking piece.

Deciding where each flower will be placed is a challenge. If you decide
before you start gluing, however, you will not be unhappy because it didn't turn
out exactly as well as you wanted it to (Fig. 3–18). Plan each side so that there is

Fig. 3–18 Delicate grasses and
leaves must be handled carefully. Decide where each piece
will be placed before gluing.

a relationship to the whole (Fig. 3–19). Each side should flow into the next as if
you laid out the four sides so that they were one flat canvas. Add petals and
flowers where needed. Cut off petals or leaves when there is too much. If you
need to fill a space consider a butterfly. Perhaps you would like to add little
animals such as a rabbit sitting under a leaf. A caterpillar climbing up a stem
might add interest. Gather all the pieces and lay them out in front of you on your
work area so that you can see what you have. Try the designs in different arrange-
ments before making the final decision as to where they will go.

Squirt some glue into a cup and add a little bit of water to thin it slightly.
Brush the glue onto the planter where the flower will be placed. Lay the design
on top of the glued area. Pat it down firmly while lifting off the excess glue with a

Fig. 3 19 Notice how the design is consistent all the way around.

damp sponge (Fig. 3–20). When gluing large flowers that are not too delicate the glue can be applied to the back of the paper and then placed onto the planter surface.

Once each side has been designed and the flowers are glued in place check over each cutout. If any of the edges are not completely secured, add a drop of glue and pat it down. All the designs should be secure before applying the varnish.

Fig. 3–20 Once glued in place the designs should be patted with a damp sponge to remove all excess glue.

For this project you will use polyurethane varnish. This is a plastic-like varnish that has an oil base and creates a very tough finish. It takes a full twenty-four hours to dry in order to assure the toughness needed for an outdoor protective surface. This is a clear finish and you should apply at least four or five coats to each side. A natural hair brush is best to use for applying the varnish. The finish will be smooth and hard. After each coat is dry sand very lightly. The surface is harder than indoor varnish and is therefore more difficult to sand smooth. After the final sanding you might want to go over the whole thing with very fine steel wool (#0000) for an extra smooth finish.

Once the sides have been completely varnished, apply a coat or two to the inside as well as the bottom. This will completely seal your planter. If you would like to add another touch, you can antique this piece. Pre-mixed antiquing is available in craft shops or you can make your own. Mix equal parts of raw umber oil paint, linseed oil and turpentine or mineral spirits. If using acrylic raw umber, mix it with a little water and nothing else. Add touches of the antique mix here and there to corners and around flowers. Wipe away the excess so that it looks natural rather than like a smudge. Use a clean soft rag to blend in the antiquing so that it looks quite natural. It will accent and highlight the designs. Add another coat of the polyurethane or varnish after you have applied the antiquing. This will protect the antique finish. Sand the last coat with a slightly wet piece of #600 sandpaper for that final glow. Apply a thin coating of clear paste wax to protect the planter and to give it a shine.

Select a plant to go into the planter that will complement rather than detract from the design. If you place a potted plant into the planter, you can change the plant with the seasons.

KEY HOLDERS

Materials Needed

small wooden plaque
design (could be a postcard; die cut shapes are used here)
white acrylic paint
scissors (if designs need to be cut out)

package of "L" hooks
brass ring for hanging
hammer and nail
#220 sandpaper
paint brush

Directions

This simple key holder can be made in less than a half hour (Fig. 3–21). You can use a wooden plaque or similar piece of scrap wood. The designs for this project can be found in bookstores or shops that sell novelty cards and wrapping paper. These designs are precut shapes which come in quite a variety of subjects: keys, cars, fruit and other simple objects. For a more elegant looking key holder, designs can be cut from prints, books, or similar sources. A favorite postcard might look nice.

Fig. 3–21 A key holder can be
a delightful yet easy project
that can be made in less than
an hour.

It will take minutes to paint the plaque and only a small jar or tube of acrylic
paint is necessary. Mix the color of your choice. This one is painted white. The
outer rim can be painted with a contrasting color. Choose a color that will be a
good background for the design you will be using. If it will hang on a wall in the
kitchen for instance, the background color should also go with your room color.

First sand the plaque or piece of wood so that it is smooth. The surface can
be painted quite quickly since it is so small. Carefully paint the edges. If you
have many keys, you should buy a larger plaque to accommodate the extra hooks.
This plaque is four inches square.

Apply two coats of paint and let each dry thoroughly. Sand the final coat so
that the surface of the plaque is once again smooth to the touch. Plan where the
designs will be placed so that they are either under each key or in such a way so
as not to be hidden by the keys. The design tells of its use. Therefore, on this
plaque, the key shape is placed where each real key will hang (Fig. 3–22). The
other examples of key holders using the free-form shapes are designed so that the
cutouts are placed in such a way as not to be hidden. This takes careful planning
so that the hooks look natural when placed in between the designs.

Once you have decided where to place the shapes, coat the entire plaque
with the polymer medium and lay the design elements on the wet surface. If the
designs are printed on heavy paper as these are, you should apply white glue to
each back and press it onto the plaque. Apply some pressure by placing a heavy
book on top of the designs while they are drying. This will keep them from
curling up. This is only necessary if the cutouts are made of cardboard as these
are.

Fig. 3–22 Die-cut shapes eliminate the need to cut out the
design. These are quite thick
and must be left to dry for a
few minutes once glued to the
plaque.

After a few minutes coat the entire plaque, design and all, with the water-base polymer medium varnish (Fig. 3–23). Really glop it on so that the designs are completely covered. This will appear murky when first applied, but will dry clear. In minutes the finish will be dry and you can apply another coat. Keep

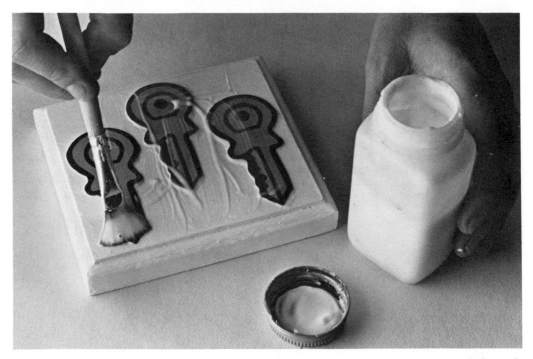

Fig. 3–23 Fast-drying water varnish is spread over the surface. At least five coats are needed to sufficiently cover the designs.

doing this until you feel that the design is covered sufficiently to protect it. No sanding is needed.

Decide where you will put the hooks. The "L" hooks are like cup hooks and are found in hardware stores. They are inexpensive and come in different lengths. The short ones are fine for this project. It is often difficult to screw something into hard wood. Therefore to make it easier, you can start the hole by hammering a nail gently into the places where you will put the hooks (Fig. 3–24).

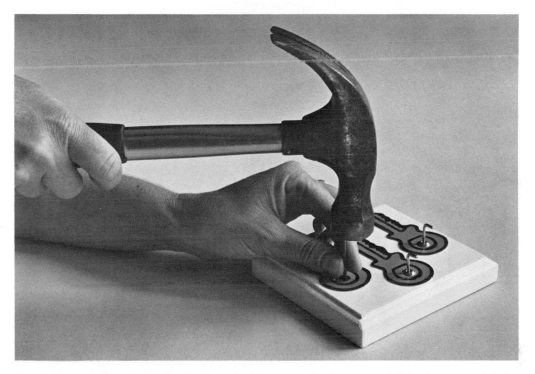

Fig. 3–24 Use a hammer and nail to get the holes started. Then screw "L" hooks into each hole. The keys will hang from these.

Just tap the nail in so that it gets started but not so hard that you can't pull it out by hand. Screw each hook into the holes that you have started. Measure across the top of the plaque to find the center. Make a hole the same way so that you can insert the brass ring for hanging. These rings are also available in hardware and some craft stores. If you would like, a piece of felt can be glued to the back for a finishing touch as well as to protect the wall.

This is such a simple project that you might suggest it for a child to make as a gift. It could also be designed with self-sticking seals that are purchased in stationery stores. An interesting postcard that is the same size as the bottom half of the plaque could be used. Simply paste the postcard to the plaque, lining it up with the sides and bottom of the plaque. Reserve the top for the hooks. If the postcard doesn't quite fit it can be trimmed or, if too small, centered.

The other key holders were cut from quarter-inch plywood using a coping saw (Figs. 3–25, 3–26). This is a small hand saw that is easy to use and is found in

Fig. 3–25 A free-form key holder can be made from ¼-inch plywood and cut with a coping saw. Designed by Ruth Linsley.

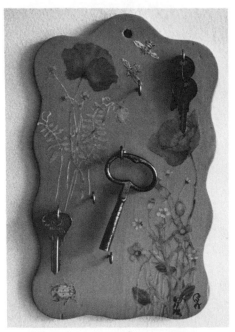

Fig. 3–26 Delicate flowers and bugs can be found in books, prints, cards, wrapping paper. Small cup hooks are used to hold the keys. Designed by Ruth Linsley.

any hardware store. The edges will be rough and in need of a good sanding to make them smooth enough to paint. For this you will need a heavy grade of sandpaper. The designs were cut from prints and flower books and the varnish is satin indoor wood oil base. This is a project that will take from seven to fourteen days and the finish will be satin smooth. If you would like to do such a project you should take time to select the designs and cut them out carefully.

CHILD'S CHAIR

Materials Needed

small child's chair (this one is made of
  plywood)
2 colors of acrylic paint
paint brush

varnish
sandpaper, #400 & #600
scissors
child's book of illustrations

Directions

Decoupage on children's furniture is an inexpensive way to personalize the child's room with an original craft idea. This child's chair is a common one used in most kindergarten classrooms (Fig. 3–27). It was found discarded in a junkyard and the only thing wrong with it was that one of the back screws was missing. The frame is made of metal and the seat and back of plywood. Perhaps you have come across a similar one. They aren't too pretty as is, but can be made to look quite attractive when decoupaged. While I chose to apply the decorations over the hole left by the missing screw, this was done out of laziness. Actually, a replacement screw could easily have been found in a hardware store. If your child has a small worktable or desk, this could be decoupaged using the same design. Do not apply the decoupage on the center or work area, but create a border around the rim and sides.

The designs for this project were all cut from one child's book found at a book fair (Fig. 3–28). The illustrations are bright and colorful. The extra flowers added here and there for interest were cut from a wildflower book. If your child has a book that has cute illustrations, this might be a good way to preserve and enjoy it long after the child has outgrown the book.

Sand the entire chair including the metal frame. If you have a similar piece of furniture that is not in perfect condition do not discard it. If there are gouges or nicks in the wood they can be filled in with wood putty. This is found in a hardware store and once applied will dry hard enough to sand smooth. It will blend right in with the surface and once painted you will not see it.

This chair is painted with an off-white acrylic paint for the seat and back. The metal frame is painted rosy pink. If you paint the background an off-white, it will create a beautiful color for almost any design. Paint the frame with a contrasting color to correspond with the child's room. Two coats of paint are applied to both sections of the chair and sanded when dry. Use #400 grit sandpaper for the pre-sanding, followed by #600 for sanding between coats of paint and varnish. If the #600 is slightly wet, it will give a smoother finish.

Fig. 3–27 A small wood and metal child's chair can make a delightful project for decoupage. The frame is painted in a contrasting color to the seat and back.

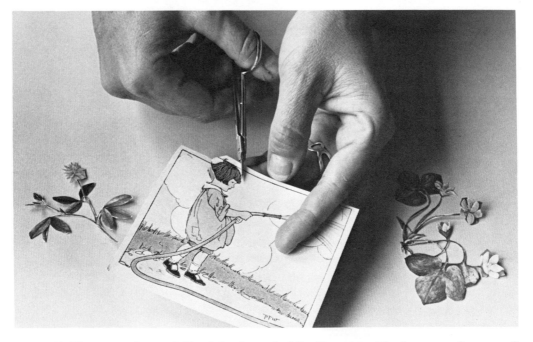

Fig. 3–28 Illustrations from a children's book are ideal for this project. The flowers are from a small paperback book of flowers and butterflies. Cut carefully, using sharp cuticle scissors.

The designs can be placed on the front and back as well as the seat if desired. Smaller cutouts such as delicate flowers are good for the narrow frame. First arrange the cutouts on the area to be covered. In this way you can decide where to fill in with flowers and leaves to give the piece a completed look. The child with the hose was cut from the edge of a page (Fig. 3–29). The hose did not continue, nor did the hose water go anywhere. Do not let a design defect deter you. Simply add to it creating your own scene. Not all design elements are complete as cut straight from the book. Often you have to improvise and this can be a lot of fun.

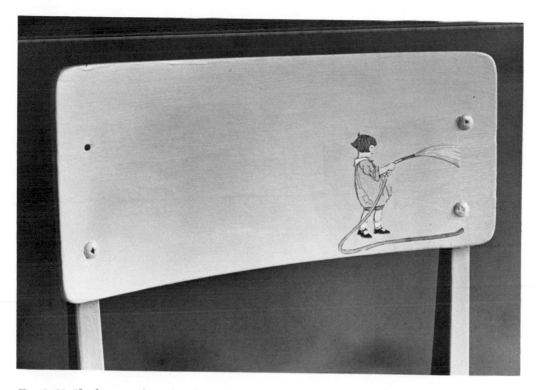

Fig. 3–29 If a design isn't perfect don't disregard it. Anything can be added or cut away to improve the illustration.

The flowers are cut and placed so that they not only cover the chopped off hose, but look quite natural under the spray of the water. The stem is placed so that it fits around the screw of the chair back (Fig. 3–30). The small flowers placed between the children and on the frame are all cut from the same source. They were selected for their brilliant colors which match the colors of the illustrations of the children.

To make placement easy, no glue is used. The back is coated with polymer medium in a glossy finish and while wet, the cutouts are pressed against the chair. This must be done immediately while the polymer is still wet. Since it dries rather quickly, it is important to know beforehand where you will place each illustration. To be sure that each one is securely glued in place, roll your brush handle over the design. This will firmly secure it as well as help to ooze out

Fig. 3–30 The flowers are placed so that they cover the end of the hose. Notice how the flowers were placed so that the stems design around the screw.

any excess medium from underneath the design. The polymer medium acts as a glue as well as a varnish. A leaf is placed over the missing screw hole (Fig. 3–31). This can be done with any imperfections. Simply design it so that a cutout covers whatever you don't want to show. When applying the polymer medium varnish, brush it on so that it doesn't create a foam. When dry, this foam will show up, will dry hard and will be impossible to sand away. Brush it on evenly so that there is no buildup in any one area.

A larger design can be used for the center of the back (Fig. 3–32). This design carries out the theme on the front. A small leaf that was left over is placed on the back of the seat. When all the designs are in place, coat the whole thing with the polymer varnish. This means the whole chair. The polymer will protect the chair from nicks and scratches when in use. Several coats can be applied as this dries almost immediately.

A glossy finish is used for this project to make it look young and new. If you apply about ten coats, the designs will become completely submerged so that they will appear to be part of the surface. This will be smooth to the touch. If you apply each coat evenly, you will find that only the slightest bit of sanding is needed between coats. Often no sanding is needed at all. The more coats of varnish that are applied, the more the surface will be protected. Small children might have a tendency to try to pull the design away from the chair. If several coats of varnish cover it, this will be impossible.

Fig. 3–31 The "scene" is complete. All these cutouts were taken from one book. The leaves at the left were placed so that they cover the hole where a screw was missing.

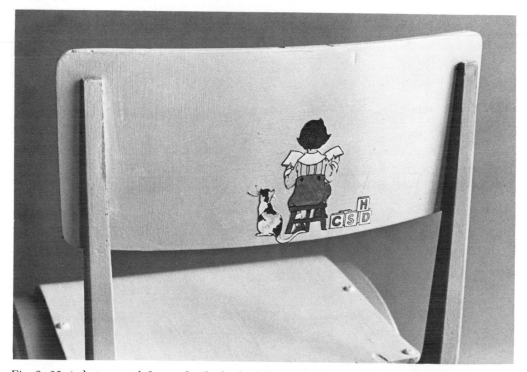

Fig. 3–32 A design was left over for the back of the chair. This completes the overall feeling.

You might find decorative letters to cut out which spell the child's name. Glue these to the back of the chair thus personalizing it. If you have wallpapered the child's room and have some left over, you might use this for some of the designs. The chair would then match the room decor.

Animals could be another design idea, or characters from a book that your child is fond of, such as Snoopy and Peanuts. Disney characters might be another consideration. Usually brightly illustrated children's books are the first to go at book fairs so if you can get to them early you might find some interesting buys.

MAIL HOLDER

Materials Needed

Wooden mail holder (or plywood and coping saw to make your own)
paint
design

brush
scissors
sandpaper, #220 and #600

Directions

This mail holder is a simple project to make (Fig. 3–33). Using quarter-inch plywood draw the pieces shown in Fig. 3–34. The pieces are cut by hand using a coping saw. Once all the pieces are cut out, they are glued together with Elmers Glue-All, then nailed with brads, which are headless nails. Set this aside to dry for a few minutes.

Fig. 3–33 A simple mail holder can be made quite easily, using 1/4-inch plywood, glue and a coping saw.

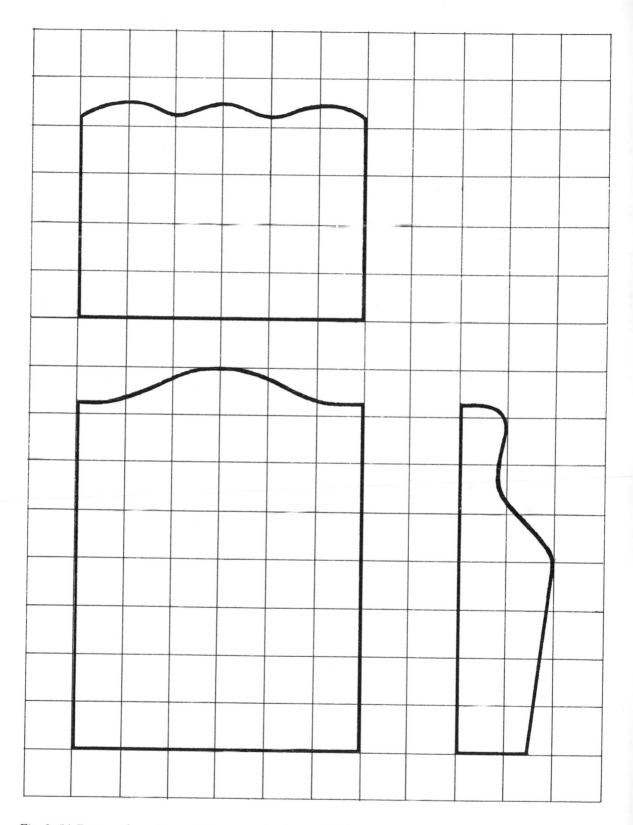

Fig. 3–34 Diagram for cutting out pieces to make the mail holder. Each square equals one inch.

41

The design for this is cut from a poster. When designing a small flat surface, it is easy to find a variety of things that can work well. Decide where you will use this project before choosing a design. While this design is kept simple, it could have had more cutouts running up the sides of the mail holder.

Once the pieces are glued and nailed together, the entire object should be sanded well (Fig. 3–35). Use a heavy duty grade of sandpaper for this. The edges

Fig. 3–35 Once put together, the wood must be sanded until smooth. Plywood is rather crude; therefore, take the time to do a good sanding job before painting.

will be quite rough and need special attention with the sandpaper. The background is deep blue acrylic paint to simulate the water. The waves of the cutout are different shades of blue which blend nicely with the background. They are outlined with a heavy black border as is the whale. The little spouts of the whale are cut out and glued in place (Fig. 3–36).

If this seems too difficult, tiny pieces like this can be painted on with a narrow artist's brush. Often the antennae of a butterfly is too delicate to cut out and must also be painted onto a surface once the wings have been glued in place.

When applying one large piece, the back should be covered adequately with glue to avoid dry spots. That is, if any part of the paper is not sufficiently coated with glue, it will appear as a large bubble when the design is glued to the surface of the object. This is difficult to remedy without ruining the piece. Be sure to coat enough glue evenly over the back.

Lay one end of the design onto the surface. With the palm of your hand smooth the design down little by little working toward the opposite outer edge. If the paper is thin, you have to be careful not to create wrinkles. This often happens when using magazine paper. As soon as the design is completely down, take your brush handle and firmly roll it across the design. Then place the brush handle in the middle of the paper and roll first to one side then to the other. If

Fig. 3–36 Two or three coats of paint are needed to cover sufficiently. The tiny whale spouts are carefully glued to the surface.

Fig. 3–37 A polyfoam brush is easy to use when applying water base varnish. Each coat will dry in five minutes and five coats should be enough.

glue oozes out of the edges, wipe it away with a damp sponge. Be sure to wipe the glue off the brush handle as well. If you forget to do this, it will stick to the paper when you roll it back again. Sometimes you run the risk of the paper sticking to the handle and pulling away. In this case, it is best if the paper is wet with glue. More is better than too little. As the paper dries, it will shrink so that it fits like skin on the surface of the mail holder.

Once the design is glued down, several coats of varnish are applied (Fig. 3–37). And that's all there is to it. Drill a hole in the center near the top so that you can hang it easily. You will have a mail holder the entire family can enjoy.

BABY BOX

Materials Needed

photograph of a baby   wrapping paper with baby theme
small box   lining paper
paint   varnish
brush   birth announcement (optional)
glue   scissors
sandpaper #220 & #600

Directions

Photographs can be used for decoupage projects and this is a lovely way to make and give a personalized gift. Birth announcement photographs, wedding pictures, graduation announcements as well as snapshots of the family can be preserved forever with decoupage. Black and white photos as well as color can be used successfully. This baby box is approximately $4^1/_2''$ x $6''$ with hinges at the back (Fig. 3–38). It is an ordinary wooden box most commonly found in craft shops. Since photographs are made on very thick paper, it often takes several coats of varnish to cover them sufficiently. It is therefore a good idea to peel a layer of paper away from the back of the photograph if at all possible.

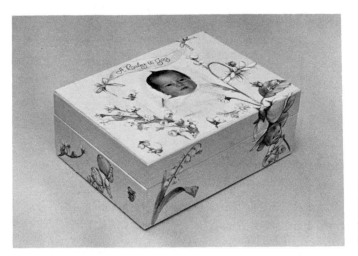

Fig. 3–38 A newborn baby's photograph is a delightful way to decoupage a keepsake box. This is an ordinary wooden box available in most craft shops.

A miniature scene can be planned using a variety of ideas. Baby wrapping paper comes in a wide assortment of designs for you to choose from. When selecting paper to use around the photograph, remember to keep it small and dainty (Fig. 3–39). Your central focus here should be on the baby's photograph and the cutouts should not be overwhelming. Usually wrapping paper for this sort of project comes in pastel colors and often delicate floral prints are available. Cut out more than you think that you'll need so that you will have enough to play around with when creating the design on the box.

Use acrylic paint in either blue, pink or yellow. Since the colors are quite intense when used right from the tube, you will need a jar or tube of white as well.

Fig. 3–39 Choose wrapping paper with delicate pastel designs and color to complement the baby's photograph. Cut extra flowers to add here and there where necessary.

Begin by preparing your box for painting. Sand the box all over, including the inside rim and the entire inside. Even though you will be lining the box, it will be a smoother job if there are no rough spots on the wood. Next squirt a tiny drop of color on a piece of paper or cardboard.

If you are doing several projects you might like to invest in a palette pad. This is a pad of wax-like paper made by Grumbacher especially for mixing paints. The paint is not absorbed into the paper and once you have used a sheet you simply tear it off and throw it away. The pad is large enough to provide you with plenty of room to mix several paints at one time.

Next to the tiny drop of acrylic color squirt a generous amount of white. Either with your brush or a palette knife mix the color into the white. Usually the tiniest drop of color is all that is needed. If your color is too dark, keep adding white until it is pale enough. The colors should be blended sufficiently before applying to the box. If the color is not mixed well, there will be streaks on your work and the color consistency will not be even. Be sure to mix enough color to cover the box completely. If you run out in the middle of painting, it is often difficult to mix and match the exact color again.

Apply the paint in one direction. If it appears to be quite thick, dip your brush into water before dipping it into the paint. Add more water if it is still too thick. The thinning will give you a smoother coat of paint and will help to avoid obvious brush strokes that are difficult to remove when sanding.

Since you will be using a pastel color, you will probably need two coats of paint on the box. Let the first coat dry completely before applying the second coat. Don't forget the inside rim when painting. Even if you will be lining the box, the inside walls should be painted a little bit. When painting the rim, extend the paint down slightly so that a little of the inside walls are painted. Then, if your paper lining isn't exactly perfect and doesn't extend right up to the edge, it will still look finished.

Sand the box after the paint has dried. Usually the inside rim needs a heavier hand with the sandpaper than the flat areas. While waiting for each coat of paint to dry, be sure to clean your brush in hot water so that it won't get stiff.

Using cuticle scissors cut the designs that you have chosen to emphasize the baby's photograph. Straight scissors can be used to trim around the photograph if this is necessary. When the paint is dry arrange the photograph on the box in different positions to see how it will best fit. If it is very small in relation to the box, you can detract from this by filling in with more cutouts. This photograph is placed right in the middle of the box with the designs overlapping the edges to soften the outline. Arrange the designs so that they generally follow the line around the photograph while slightly overlapping here and there.

The good thing about using wrapping paper for the cutouts rather than a greeting card is that there is always enough to use if you find that you need a little addition here and there. The second advantage is that greeting card paper is quite thick (like the photographic paper), creating too great a thickness when overlapping the two. The wrapping paper is very thin, therefore just right for using over parts of the photograph.

Once you are sure where the basic cutouts will go, you can glue them in place and then add details. It is best to add a little at a time. First center the photograph. Apply plenty of glue to the back, but not so much that you will have most of it oozing out of the sides. Let the glue set for about one minute before placing the photograph on the box. It is all right for a black and white photograph to get wet; but if you are rubbing over a color photo, you run the risk of wiping away some of the color (Fig. 3–40). A black and white photograph can be presoaked in water before gluing and then placed on the box. Pat the excess water away with a dry towel. As the photograph dries it will shrink and fuse with the box top. Do not do this with a color photo however. Let the photograph set on the box for a few minutes before applying the rest of the designs. If some of the

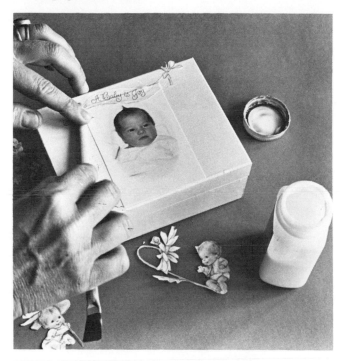

Fig. 3–40 Once the photograph is glued to the top of the box roll the brush handle over it to force excess glue out from under the picture. This will secure the photograph so that it will not lift.

cutouts are glued so that they cover the opening, wait for them to dry before cutting with a razor blade. Wrapping paper is thin and can rip easily if not dry before pulling the razor across the middle of it.

When gluing down these delicate designs, be sure that your hands are clean so that they will not stick to your cutouts in handling (Fig. 3–41). Be sure that your sponge is only slightly damp when patting each design. Do not wipe across the cutouts. This may cause them to wrinkle and pull away from the surface.

If you are anxious to give this gift to someone right away, you should use the

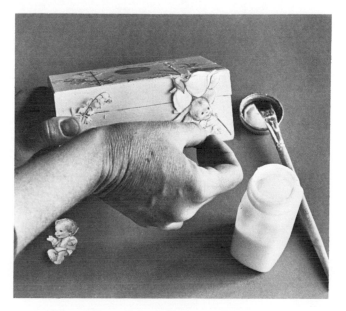

Fig. 3–41 Plan the designs and handle them carefully when gluing. This paper is thin and will rip easily.

water varnish. If you would like to coat the box so that the photograph is completely sunken under the varnish, use indoor wood, semi-gloss or satin finish varnish. This should be applied with a natural hair brush in thin rather than thick coats so that it will not drip while drying. Brush the varnish onto each flat area in one direction (Fig. 3–42). With the very tip of your brush, draw it across each section in the opposite direction. Then set the box aside.

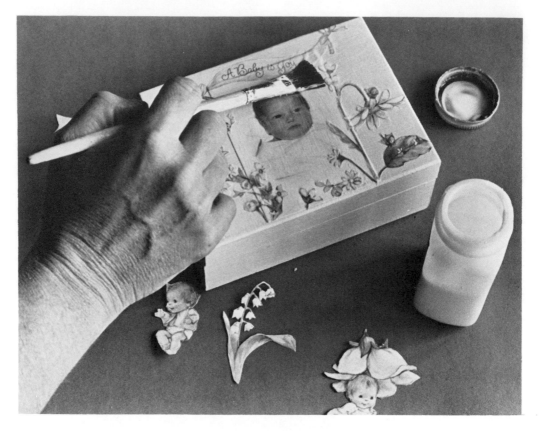

Fig. 3–42 Brush the varnish right across the box once the designs are in place. Water varnish will dry quickly, but an oil-base varnish will give a smoother finish to the surface.

While each coat dries, your brush will be kept soft if suspended in a jar of brush cleaner. A clip-type clothes pin is perfect for securing your brush just above the lid of the jar. This will hold your brush up so that the bristles do not rest on the bottom of the jar or can, thus causing it to curl.

Before sanding this piece, there should be at least three or four coats of varnish on it. When sanding, do it gently with a very light hand. This will prevent you from sanding away any of the designs since the photograph is raised. Apply a little more varnish around the edges of the photograph when applying the first few coats. Continue to apply coats of varnish until the design is sufficiently submerged under it. There will be a slightly raised feeling when you run your hand over the surface, but this adds to the interest. Texture in your work is more interesting than a completely flat piece.

The inside can be lined with more of the wrapping paper or another complementary design (Fig. 3–43). Perhaps you would like to line it with fabric. Check the directions for the sewing box to see how to line with fabric. If you line the box with paper, you can add the birth announcement inside the lid of the box. Completely line the box including the part that will be covered. Cut the announcement to fit inside and apply glue to the back of it. Place it into the lid. Using a solid object that will fit inside, press over the entire card. For instance, using a butter knife, smooth along the edges and down the middle of the announcement to be sure that there are no trapped air bubbles. This will ensure that when the announcement is dry it will be smooth.

Once again, using the varnish, coat the entire inside. Brush the varnish over the rim of the box as well as any areas that have been covered with paper. You may want to apply several coats of varnish to the announcement, but only one coat is necessary for the rest of the inside.

You can either glue a piece of the matching greeting paper to the bottom or cut a piece of felt in a color that picks up one of the colors from the design. Place the box right on the felt and draw a line around it using a pencil. Cut this piece out. Apply glue to the bottom of the box so that there is no excess. You don't want any glue to get on the outside of the felt. Lay the piece of felt on the bottom and smooth it out with a knife or your brush handle. If there is any edge of excess felt showing, trim this with a razor blade or your cuticle scissors.

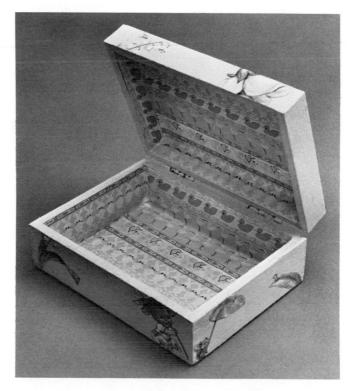

Fig. 3–43 A subtle wrapping paper with small designs is used to line the baby box. Apply a coat or two of varnish to protect the lining.

SLAT TABLE

Materials Needed

inexpensive fold-up slat table   scissors
paint   bird print
sandpaper #220 and #400 or #600   glue
brush   wax
varnish (indoor wood oil-base)   rag
brush cleaner

Directions

The table used for this project is a small occasional, fold-up table that is found in variety stores. It is quite inexpensive and comes in a natural blond wood, often coated with a thin layer of shellac (Fig. 3–44). This project is particularly interesting because it presents a design challenge. It must be done with regular, long-drying varnish because it will probably be in constant use. It may even be used outdoors on a patio. Shellac or lacquer will not protect this surface, nor will the quick-drying varnish. The only coating that will be completely mar and stain-proof is long-drying, wood varnish. This finish is matte. It is also antiqued, which is an optional detail applied only at the very end.

First the table is sanded. If all exposed areas are not well sanded, the paint will not adhere to the surface. This sanding is all that is needed to remove any wax or shellac that might coat the surface. Off-white acrylic paint is used on this

Fig. 3–44 This small wooden occasional table is available in variety stores and is quite inexpensive. It presents a design challenge.

table. Use a background color that will set off your design. The print for this table is from an oversized book of bird prints. The brilliant green of the leaves is emphasized against the off-white background.

When selecting a print for this type of object, be sure that it is large enough to span the entire surface. Remember also that the design will be cut apart, therefore it will appear smaller when on a page in a book. If the original print, before it is cut up, is the same size as the table top, it will be too large for this project unless part of it can be cut away.

A delicate print is ideal for this project. Use your cuticle scissors for cutting. Cut parts of the print that are most difficult to handle, then finish with the larger sections, such as the bird.

Once the entire print has been cut out, place it on top of the table (Fig. 3–45). This will give you an idea as to where it will be cut apart. Adjust it so that

Fig. 3–45 Cut out a delicate design using cuticle scissors. Lay the design across the table before cutting it to fit.

it will not be split at awkward points. When you know exactly how it will be, do not remove it. Using a straight scissors, cut the print apart between the first and second slit (Fig. 3–46). Lift this first part of the design. Mix a little water with the white glue in a cup. Thin the glue slightly so that you can brush it onto the table. With your paintbrush, apply the glue mixture onto the first slat where the design will be. Carefully lay the design piece on top of this glued area. Wet a sponge and press down firmly on top of the design so that much of the excess glue on the table is removed while you secure the print. Use a knife to press the overlap against the inside of the slat. Continue to apply the rest of the design in this way.

Fig. 3–46 Cut between each slat as you glue the pieces in place. A butter knife helps to press the design against the inside between the slats as they are glued.

Before gluing each successive piece be sure to line it up correctly so that, while there are spaces between the design, it is still perfectly matched. Save a little extra leaf here and there for the legs of the table. If you have a lot more you can elaborate on the design by having vines twine around the legs. If there is only a little left, it is best to use the extra sparingly rather than to add material from another print. In this way the entire design will blend together.

Be sure to check each of the design elements to see that all edges are securely glued down. When varnishing, the sides of each slat should be coated, as well as the undersides if this table will be used outdoors. When varnishing an object like this, it is often hard to see all the areas and often a spot or two is overlooked. If you place the table so that you are varnishing against the light, you will have a reflection where you have applied varnish. In this way you will know if you have missed anything. It will take about six coats of varnish to sufficiently protect this surface so that you can feel free to place drinks on it without fear of harm. After the second or third coat has dried completely, you can begin to sand between each successive coating with #400 or #600 sandpaper.

If you decide to antique, this can be a nice added touch and is done after the final varnishing. Do not sand the last coat of varnish if you intend to antique. The antique mix can be purchased pre-mixed or you can make your own. (See

Multicolored Egg

Pressed Flower Candle

Wooden Catchall

Sewing Box

Catchall Buckets

Child's Chair

Repoussé Collage

Rocks and Shells

Birthday Calendar

Cable Spool Table

Baby's Box

Mail Holder

Slat Table

Tin Planter

Outdoor Planter

Snax Stuffers

Tin Can Planters

Chapter 2.) A raw umber or earth tone gives the nicest antiqued effect. Do each section or slat at a time. Brush the mix right onto the surface. Using a clean soft cloth, wipe away most of the antiquing, leaving a little here and there for accent. The antique mix should remain in corners and around the details of the designs. This will be a nice accent for the design elements. The antiquing should achieve a subtle effect. Do not simply brush the antiquing across the print, leaving it there to dry in streaks. Wipe away most of what you put on. If you don't like the effect, simply remove it at once.

It is necessary to work with each section at a time so that the antique mix won't dry on your piece in areas that will not look well. Once the entire piece is antiqued, leave it to dry for several hours. After that you will apply a last and protective coat of varnish over all. When this has dried, sand it lightly. Dip the sandpaper in soapy water for the last sanding. For an even smoother finish, top off the final sanding by rubbing over the surface with #0000 steel wool.

Brush away any steel wool or sanding paste created by the wet sanding and apply a coat of clear furniture paste wax. Butcher's Bowling Alley Wax will give your piece a lasting and beautiful finish. Every six months an application of wax will help to preserve the lovely finish that you have created.

CABLE SPOOL TABLE

Materials Needed

large cable spool (used for telephone and cable wire)

piece of balsa wood (large enough to cover each hole in top)

3M Super Strength glue

X-Acto knife

small can of wood putty

heavy duty sandpaper (or electric hand sander)

large poster design

scissors

enamel paint

large paintbrush (2″ or more)

quart of polyurethane

glue (white)

rolling pin or brayer

brush cleaner

Directions

A cable spool makes an excellent outdoor table. These spools are usually used to hold telephone, cable or television wire and electrical cable. In some parts of the country they can be found in abundance. Often they are discarded at local dumps, or are left in fields to rot. In other parts of the country they are extremely hard to obtain because they are in such demand. I have even heard of people stopping the workers putting up telephone wires to secure the spool when they have finished. However, they are available and they do come in all sizes.

Most of the spools are not in very good condition and need a bit of restoration work before starting (Fig. 3–47). Sometimes they have gouges and rotted areas that must be sanded and filled in. This can be done easily enough with wood putty. The most bothersome problems are the large knotholes and bolts, as well as the center hole. These must be dealt with before applying any print.

Fig. 3–47 An old electrical cable spool can be restored and decoupaged for an elegant outdoor table.

To prepare this object you will first do a lot of sanding. If you have an electric sander you can use it. However, a sanding object that holds strips of sandpaper makes hand sanding much easier. This is available in some craft shops and almost all hardware stores. There is a lightweight plastic one made by the 3M Company. For this you will use heavy duty sandpaper. If there is paint on the spool that you find, it should be removed. Any commercial paint remover can be purchased in a hardware store. A paint scraper will come in handy as well. This work should be done outdoors. If you cannot work outside, spread lots of newspaper on the floor and open the windows.

If the spool has been outside for any length of time it may be wet inside the wood. These cable spools are not made of very hard wood and absorb moisture. Leave it for a couple of days, even longer if possible, in the sun and raised off the ground. If indoors, place in a dry area, perhaps near a radiator. If the wood is wet the paint will peel off easily.

The next problem to tackle is those bolts and holes. Wood putty, as mentioned before, can be used to fill in gouges and holes. It is also used to fill in the recessed areas around the bolts. The putty comes in a small can and you will use only a small amount. Use a flat stick, such as one from an ice cream pop, to apply this. If you have nothing else, use a screwdriver, but be sure to clean it well before the putty hardens on it. Fill in these areas so that they are flush with the surface of the top. Leave this overnight to dry. When it is hard, you can sand it smooth with the heavy sandpaper.

To fill in the holes use balsa wood. This is soft wood used for building models and is found in craft and hobby shops or toy stores. It comes in strips. Be sure to buy a piece that is wide enough to fit the hole.

Using a piece of tracing paper, lay it on top of the hole and draw a circle that is the same size. Place this tracing on top of the balsa wood and using a pin make holes around the circle right through the paper to the balsa wood. Remove the paper and draw a circle connecting the dots on the balsa. The best way to cut out the balsa wood circle is with an X-Acto knife. This can be purchased at a craft, toy or art supply store.

Once the circle is cut, it will probably be a little bit larger than the hole. Sand around the edges until it fits snuggly. To secure it permanently, apply 3M Super Strength glue around the inside rim of the hole. Then apply the glue around the edge of the balsa wood circle. Force fit the piece in place so that it is flush with the top of the table. Let this dry for several hours before painting.

This project requires outdoor paint such as flat enamel (Fig. 3–48). For this you will need a brush cleaner such as turpentine or mineral spirits. If you use a dark color, one coat should cover sufficiently. This cable spool is painted with burnt orange. It will take at least a quart of paint to cover the entire table with two coats.

Fig. 3–48 Once sanded, the holes are filled with balsa wood. The table is given a coat of outdoor paint. Sometimes more than one coat is needed to sufficiently cover the surface.

The poster for this project is a sunflower print purchased at the New York Botanical Garden gift shop (Fig. 3–49). When choosing a design, posters are a good source for objects that are as large as this. Use suitable scissors to cut out the designs that will be used. Gluing a large design to a flat surface can be tricky. Open the bottle of glue and pour enough glue into the center of the table to form

Fig. 3–49 Posters are large enough to be used as decoupage designs for furniture. This bright yellow sunflower is a poster from The Brooklyn Botanical Gardens in New York.

a small puddle. Wet a rag and use it to spread the glue to the outer edges of the table (Fig. 3–50).

Decide where to place the design. Carefully lift the cutout design and place the top edge onto the table. Hold the other end of the poster design in one hand while you begin to smooth the design down with the other (Fig. 3–51). Once the poster is completely pressed down onto the surface, use a rolling pin to smooth out wrinkles and bumps. Start at the center and roll toward the outer edges (Fig. 3–52). This will force the excess glue out while smoothing down the design. Go over and over the paper with the rolling pin. Press down with your weight as you roll. If some of the design overlaps onto the edges, be sure that it is secure. This should be left to dry for at least an hour.

Polyurethane is best for covering this object. Begin with the base and work up to the top. Apply a coat around the top rim. Do not use an excess of liquid or it will drip. Dip your brush directly into the can and float the polyurethane across the top of the table. Put plenty in the center and from there spread the polyurethane to the outer edges so that the liquid thins out as you spread it. This will take all day to dry, often a full twenty-four hours. It is best therefore to coat the table in the morning so that it will be fairly dry by evening. Because it takes so long, and if it is done outdoors, it is hard to keep the finish free from dirt particles in the air. Once the finish is dry these imperfections can be sanded down with fine, black sandpaper. Apply at least three coats of polyurethane before

Fig. 3–50 With a damp cloth spread the glue over the entire tabletop. Be sure that there are no dry areas. There should be plenty of glue spread evenly over all parts that will be decoupaged.

Fig. 3–51 Excess paper areas are cut away before applying the design. Smooth it carefully as it is applied. There should be no wrinkles or bumpy areas.

Fig. 3–52 A rolling pin is perfect for smoothing down the design. This will eliminate any air bubbles trapped under the paper.

Fig. 3–53 For added interest the piece can be antiqued. This is done by painting the antique mix onto a small area at a time and wiping away most of it. The antique that is left should be blended in and around the design with a clean cloth. Do a small area at a time until done.

using the table. The finish can be waxed with furniture paste wax in order to give it a satin shine.

If you will be using this table inside, you can use a regular indoor wood or decoupage varnish and apply it the same way. The underside of the tabletop should be varnished in order to prevent moisture from getting into the wood.

For an unusual look, the table can be antiqued, doing a small area at a time until complete (Fig. 3–53).

4

Decoupage On Metal

Decoupage can be applied to metal surfaces in almost the same way as wood. Acrylic paint covers the surface just fine. There are several paints that are recommended especially for painting on metal, one of which is Rust-oleum which prevents the metal from rusting. However, for the most part, decoupage projects are small and used exclusively as indoor objects and do not need this special paint. The decoupage process can also be applied right to the metal surface without the preparation of a coat of paint.

If you have a badly rusted metal object that you would like to use, the rust must first be removed. Do not paint right over the rust. This is easily removed with a bit of sanding unless it has done extensive damage. Then you will have to use a rust remover.

Many of the throw-away objects found around the home are made of metal and are perfect for decoupage containers, the most common being a metal or tin can. Since there are all kinds of sizes and shapes their use can be limitless (Fig. 4–2). Makes a pencil caddy, planters, a candle holder or a catch-all for the kitchen or a desk. Band-aid boxes are perfect for children's crayons or paper clips. Aspirin tins can be designed and used as pill containers. Sand pails are fine for holding a variety of things.

The only preparation for doing a project on metal is sanding. If a metal item is first sanded, the paint will have a better surface to sink into. When painting do not go over the same spot twice as you will pull the paint away.

Fig. 4–1 This tin planter is decoupaged with pressed flowers and paper butterflies.

PRESSED FLOWER DECOUPAGE

Materials Needed

tin planter   brush cleaner
acrylic paint   •   pressed flowers
brush   antique mix (optional)
sandpaper (medium and fine)   scissors
varnish   paper butterfly designs (optional)

Directions

Old, often rusty tin containers can be found in junk shops. Some plant and florist shops sell metal or tin planters. These can be used in the conventional way by decorating with cutout flowers and butterflies or you might like to try applying pressed, real flowers (Fig. 4–1). A pressed flower design can correspond with the same plant that is held in the container.

You should plan this project a week before you actually begin to allow time to press a few flowers. Of course, if you already have some pressed you can begin at once.

Depending on the time of year, pick a variety of flowers that are not too pulpy. Marigolds, buttercups, dogwood and violets as well as many weeds are excellent for pressing. For this project you will not need many but it is a good idea

Fig. 4–2 Metal and tin containers are exciting projects for decoupage. Look for interesting shapes and sizes. They can often be found in junk shops.

to have more than you will actually use. In this way you will have a variety to choose from, or you can save them for future projects.

Pick the flowers and place each on a paper towel. Be sure that they do not touch one another. Lay another piece of paper toweling on top of the flowers. Place a heavy book on top of the towel. The paper toweling absorbs the moisture in the flowers to help dry them out. Place several books on top of one another and leave for a week. In this way the flowers will become dried out, pressed flat, yet they will retain their color.

If the planter is rusty or simply old and dirty, wash it first. Then, using a medium grade sandpaper, such as a #320, sand all exposed areas thoroughly (Fig. 4–3). After this you can give the planter a coat of acrylic paint in the color of your choice. Paint the outside and the exposed rim, but not the inside (Fig. 4–4). When selecting a color, choose one that will create a complementary background for the flowers that you have pressed. This planter is sunshine yellow. Since paint does not adhere to metal as well as it does to wood, be careful when sanding. Once the paint is dry, you can sand the surface lightly and then apply a second coat. Again, when sanding, do it carefully.

Before actually applying the pressed flowers to the surface, try arranging them in different ways. Handle your pressed flowers delicately. They may need trimming or cutting apart to make them fit the way you would like (Fig. 4–5).

Fig. 4–3 A dirty old metal container can be sanded so that the surface is clean and ready to be painted.

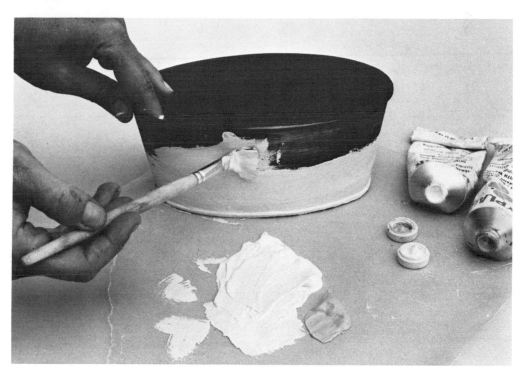

Fig. 4–4 Mix acrylic paints to the color that will best complement the plant and design that will be used.

Since they are dried and stiff once they are ready for use, you have to cut apart and rearrange when you want them to bend this way or that.

Squirt the glue right from the bottle onto the planter. Put plenty of glue in the area where you will place the first flower. Lay the flower right down on top of

Fig. 4–5 Snip pressed flowers so that they can be arranged in a pleasing way on the container.

Fig. 4–6 Apply enough glue to the surface so that the flower will adhere when placed on it. The excess glue can then be patted away with a damp sponge.

the glue and press it there by using a damp sponge (Fig. 4–6). Keep applying the flowers this way until your design is complete. Do not be afraid to use plenty of glue. Once all the designs have been placed on top of the glue, you can pat the excess away as best you can. If you want to add some touches to the design, such as a butterfly, you might cut one from paper and glue it in place (Fig. 4–7).

When varnishing the surface, lay the planter on its side so that the varnish will not drip down the front. Dip your brush into the varnish and apply it, almost in puddles, around the flowers. Then spread it across the surface area between

Fig. 4–7 Additional design elements can be cut from paper. These butterflies are from a page of a book.

the designs (Fig. 4–8). Let this dry in an out-of-the-way place. You will have to apply several coats of varnish in this way. Do not attempt to submerge the flowers completely under varnish so that you have an absolutely smooth surface. Do not sand this either. The varnish will protect the flowers and they will look lovely and interesting under the coats of varnish.

Fig. 4–8 Several coats of varnish will preserve the flowers. Once several coats have dried the additional paper designs can be added. Or you can place them down before varnishing.

Sometimes dust and specks of the dried flowers dry on the varnished surface. If you antique this project, it will camouflage this. Apply a bit of antiquing here and there, mostly in and around the flowers (Fig. 4–9). With a clean rag

Fig. 4–9 A touch of antiquing around the flowers adds interest as well as covering up any imperfections in the surface.

Fig. 4–10 Wipe away most of the antiquing, leaving enough around the flowers for accent. It should not look muddy. An earth tone will look best.

wrapped around your finger, rub away most of the antiquing, leaving a smoky outline (Fig. 4–10). Set this aside to dry for a couple of hours. Once dry, apply a last coat of varnish.

Choose a small plant that would look nice in the planter. Be sure that it isn't one that has heavy hanging leaves or they will hide the design on the front. Perhaps you will fill it with dirt and plant some seeds. Obviously this is not a one-day project, but it is a lovely way to fix up an old planter.

TIN CAN PLANTERS

Materials Needed

cans of all sizes (any kind of can)
different colors of acrylic paint
brush
scissors
sandpaper

wrapping paper
pre-stick seals (or decals)
rub-on transfers
polymer medium (glossy)

Fig. 4–11 Cans of all sizes can be used for decoupage. Save several to do at once.

Directions

Don't throw away your cans! Soup cans, fruit cans, vegetable cans, large cans, small tomato paste cans, orange juice cans, all make wonderful plant holders (Fig. 4–15). They can be easily and quickly decoupaged. They can be lined up on a window sill. They can be hung in windows. If you need a gift within the hour, you can whip up a fabulous decoupaged planter. A planter like this is great to sell at a fund-raising function. Kids can make them for gifts, for school or to decorate their rooms. Since you will be using such an inexpensive material to begin with, this kind of project calls for simple, inexpensive designs. It can be quite satisfying to make something very quickly, get professional looking results and not have it cost much. So start collecting cans.

Paint the cans in different acrylic colors. Try to do this neatly so that you won't have to sand the surface and only one coat will be sufficient. When the paint is dry, coat each can with polymer medium. The shiny finish looks best on the cans. This coat of water varnish will protect the paint from peeling away since it does not adhere as well to metal as to wood. Once the paint is protected with the varnish, it will be easier to handle the project. This will take less than five minutes to dry.

Wrapping paper provides an endless supply of designs to use. Perhaps a couple of the cans could have some cutouts from a sheet of wrapping paper. Self-sticking seals are available from variety stores and there is a lot to choose from (Fig. 4–12). Fruits and vegetables, flags, flowers, leaves, birds, hearts and cartoon characters are but a few of the subjects. Simply peel off the seal and place it in the center of the can. Press and it is applied. A sheet of butterflies provides the added touch for one of the cans used here (Fig. 4–13). Rub-on transfers are good to use if you would like the delicate designs of a flower but don't want to take the time to cut it out (Fig. 4–14). These are available in a variety of subjects

Fig. 4–12 Paint the cans with acrylic paint in a variety of colors. Pre-stick seals are a quick and easy way to design them.

Fig. 4–13 Pre-cut butterflies
eliminate cutting. The flower
design is a rub-on transfer. You
cannot tell that it has not been
carefully cut out with the cuticle scissors.

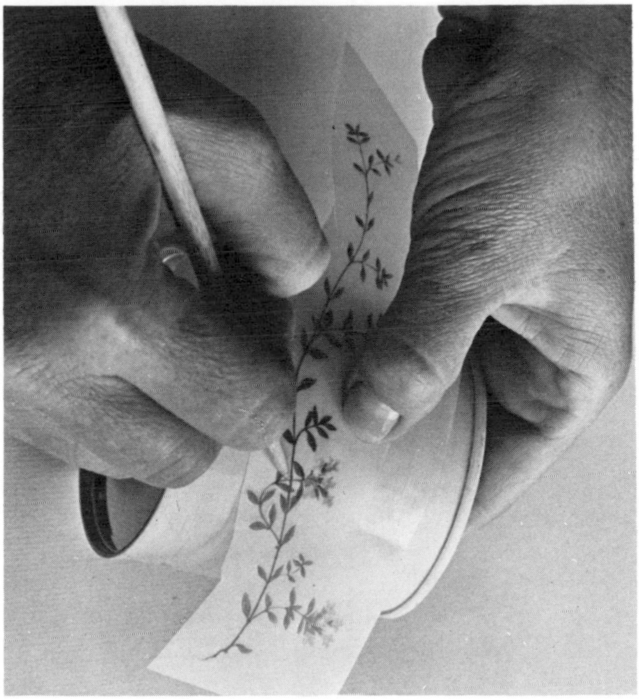

Fig. 4–14 A rub-on transfer
design makes it a snap to create
a lovely decoupage project. The
designs available are limited,
however.

from a craft or toy store. Made by Letraset or Heirloom, this is a design that is
placed on the object and, using a solid object such as a brush handle, is rubbed
onto the surface. It will adhere and look as though the design had been cut out
and glued onto the can.

Fig. 4–15 Ordinary paint, juice, and vegetable cans are turned into lovely, easy to make, decoupage planters.

    Once all the cans have been designed, they can be varnished. It is a good idea to make several at one time since it doesn't take that much longer than it takes to do one. Use the glossy polymer medium with a polyfoam brush. This will avoid the brush strokes so that you won't have to do much sanding. Brush the varnish over the exposed surface of all cans. Spread only a small amount with your brush, or it will dry in spots that will look like hard foam. When this polymer medium is first applied, it will appear white and murky while wet. As it dries it will become clear. Apply several coats, allowing each to dry before applying another. Three coats should be fine and will take fifteen minutes from start to finish.

    Fill each can with a small plant and you will have a delightful array of springtime containers (Fig. 4–15).

HAPPY BIRTHDAY DECOUPAGE

Materials Needed

paint can
birthday wrapping paper
paint, two different colors
polymer medium

sponge
colored tissue paper
fresh flowers

Fig. 4–16 A rose-colored paint can is turned into a birthday present using wrapping paper designs.

Fig. 4–17 Cut out the design so that it fits the area to be covered.

Directions

If you are going to a birthday party and need a quick, personal gift, here is a suggestion (see Fig. 4–20). Save one of the cans that you have painted. This one is rose-colored pink which is a mixture of white and cadmium red acrylic paint. The can is a quart-size paint can. Using birthday wrapping paper, cut out some of the flowers as well as the "happy birthday" (Fig. 4–16). Cut the designs so that they will fit comfortably on the can (Fig. 4–17). Snip away any excess paper.

Next apply a coat of polymer medium (water varnish) and before it dries lay each cutout right on top of it. If the varnish begins to dry while you are arranging the cutouts, apply more. The paper is so thin that the varnish can be used as the glue. Using a damp sponge, pat each design in place (Fig. 4–18). Apply another coat of the varnish over the entire design (Fig. 4–19). When this dries apply

Fig. 4–18 A damp sponge wipes away any excess glue.

Fig. 4–19 Water varnish in a glossy finish is perfect for this project. Three or four coats will dry quickly leaving a smooth shiny finish.

Fig. 4–20 Fill the birthday can with fresh cut flowers or a small planter and take to the party. Or it could be a party centerpiece.

another coat. This will create a protective, shiny finish. Pick some flowers or, if it is winter time, buy a bunch of delicate flowers and arrange them in the can (Fig. 4–20). Wrap a piece of colored tissue paper over the whole thing, just as a florist does with a bouquet of flowers, and take this gift to the party.

When the flowers die, the can can be used for a small plant or as a catch-all to hold pencils. It will be a constant reminder to the receiver of your thoughtfulness.

COOKIE CANNISTER

Materials Needed

large cannister
sandpaper #320 and #600
brush
black acrylic paint
varnish
children's book of illustrations or similar
    design source
scissors

glue
wrapping paper for lining
brush cleaner (if using oil-base varnish)
stencil
pastel color paint
pencil and ruler
fine-pointed artist's paintbrush

Directions

Large old cannisters are sometimes available in junk or antique shops. Perhaps you have one tucked away. This one is made of metal and was used for sugar (Fig. 4–21). It is quite large and obviously used in the days when sugar was a lot cheaper than it is today. If you cannot find one as nice as this one, perhaps you can find a smaller container such as a coffee can with a plastic lid. An old square cannister could work just as well. The project is shown in Fig. 4–26.

Fig. 4–21 Old cannisters and other odds and ends can be found almost anywhere. Look in your garage or attic for a forgotten object.

If you find a nice but dented metal container begin by getting it into shape. Hammer the dents out from the inside. Sand off the old finish as best you can (Fig. 4–22). It doesn't have to be a perfect job. The sanding will remove old paint and will prepare the metal surface for a new coat of paint.

A flat black acrylic paint is a good background color for most illustrations (Fig. 4–23). This can give your piece a dramatic feeling. Black will cover any surface in one coat. It will also help to minimize any dents or imperfections. Paint all exposed areas in one direction. It is easy to coat something with black paint because it covers so well. Wash the paintbrush until no traces of the black paint are left. If you will be using this same brush for varnishing, you will see streaks of black in the varnish if the brush is not absolutely clean.

Do not sand this surface. Choose designs that are large enough for the ob-

Fig. 4–22 Use heavy sand-
paper to remove an old finish.

Fig. 4–23 A coat of acrylic
paint can restore the finish of
the worst looking object.

ject. A children's book can provide the necessary cutouts. You will be able to create a scene that is consistent all the way around by using the designs from one source. A children's scene is appropriate for a cookie cannister. However, you could consider using a floral design. Select flower prints that are large enough so that the flowers can be placed around the bottom and will extend up the sides all the way around. This could be a pleasing design with a whimsical feeling. Bright colors will look best against the black background. Avoid dark green leaves and stems. The clown that is used on this cannister is wearing a red and white suit. The designs can be rather large and therefore quite easy to cut out. A flower or some grass pieces add a touch here and there to the bottom.

Cut each design out carefully. Cuticle scissors are best for any cutting, especially when it is necessary to get into tiny areas (Fig. 4–24). Cut away all excess paper even if it means cutting away a little of the edges of the designs.

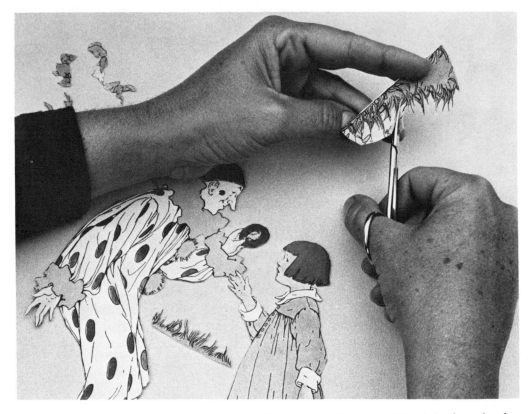

Fig. 4–24 Cuticle scissors are used to cut out delicate designs. Look for children's books with colorful illustrations.

This is better than leaving a ragged edge all the way around. Be sure that you have cut enough of a design to create a scene that will extend all the way around the cannister (Fig. 4–25). Try to avoid unrelated designs. It will be interesting if this design can tell a story. Before gluing each piece in place, decide where each will go. Squirt a small amount of glue in the middle of the back of one of the cutouts. Spread the glue to all outer edges. Place the design on the cannister in the

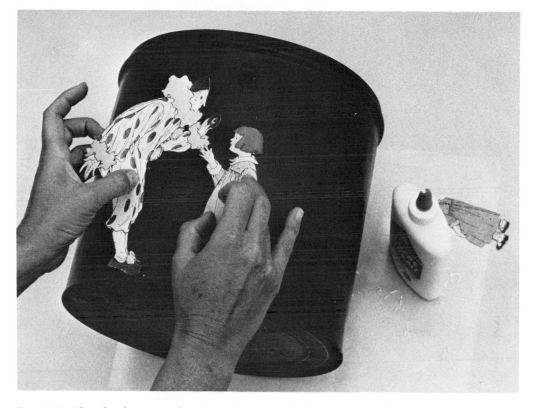

Fig. 4–25 Glue the designs so that they tell a story all the way around the cannister. Be sure that all edges are securely glued to the surface.

exact spot planned for it. Press it down with the palm of your hand. Hold one hand inside the cannister and press against it with the other against the design piece. Using the brush handle, roll over the cutout that you have just glued. This is especially important on a round object. With a flat surface the designs are more secure once glued in place. Roll over the design several times and wipe away excess glue with a damp sponge.

Continue to apply all the cutouts in this manner. Check each one to be sure that there are no raised edges. It will take a couple of minutes for the glue to dry under the paper cutouts.

If you decide to use polymer medium varnish for this project, it will be possible to finish it in a day. However, the long-drying indoor wood varnish will provide a smoother, longer-lasting finish which is completely waterproof, unlike the water varnish. This may be an important factor for a cannister that will be handled often. It can be sponged clean if you use the oil-base varnish. If you would like a very glassy finish which is quite contemporary looking, use the glossy varnish. For a matte look, use a satin or matte indoor wood varnish (Fig. 4–26). These are all available in craft shops.

Several coats of varnish are necessary to cover the designs. Apply the varnish with a natural hair varnish brush that is approximately one-half or one inch wide. Dip the brush into the varnish can and wipe the excess off on the inside

Fig. 4–26 Indoor wood varnish is applied over all. This must dry for twenty-four hours. Five or more coats are used.

rim. Start at the top of the can and brush the varnish toward the bottom of the cannister. Be sure to coat the cannister all the way around, not missing a spot. If the coating is thin, the varnish will not drip down the side. If this happens there will be dried drip marks on the finished piece. Allow this to dry overnight before applying another coat. After three coats of varnish, sand the entire piece very lightly with the #600 sandpaper. This will remove any dust or dirt particles that may have dried on the varnish finish. Continue to coat the cannister two or three more times, allowing each coat to dry before sanding again. If you have decided to use the polymer medium, five or six coats of varnish can be applied within a half hour.

This cannister is lined with pink and white polka dot wrapping paper. Since wrapping paper is quite thin, it will take extra care when handling and gluing such large pieces. Measure the height of the cannister and mark this on the paper (Fig. 4–27). Lay the cannister at one edge of the paper and wrap the paper around the outside to determine how large a piece to cut for the inside wall. Cut this piece. If it is a little larger than you think will be needed, this is fine. The paper may shrink a little when it is glued to the inside of the cannister. If there is a bit left at the top it can later be trimmed with a razor blade.

Next draw a circle around the bottom and cut this piece out for the inside bottom lining. If this is a little bit larger than the actual inside, it will fit better.

Fig. 4–27 Pink and white polka dot wrapping paper is used for the lining.

There will be enough so that you can really push it into the edges. Since this piece will be glued in position first, any excess that comes up onto the sides will be covered. Cut another piece of wrapping paper for the inside top and the inside top rim.

It will be easier to line the container if you apply the glue directly to the inside wall of the bottom half. Thin the glue slightly by dipping your brush in water, then use it to spread the glue all over the inside. Insert the wrapping paper that you have cut for this. With the cannister on the table, press it against your body. With your hands inside the cannister, you will then be able to press and smooth the paper inside as you turn it around. When applying the bottom piece, put the glue on the bottom and lay the paper into the bottom of the cannister. Press it down as smoothly as possible so that no bubbles or creases appear. The top is done in this same way. Let this dry for a couple of minutes. As the glue dries under the paper it will tighten and a few imperfections will disappear.

Apply a coat of varnish to the inside. Leave the top open when drying (Fig. 4–28). A second coat of varnish should be all that is needed to protect the lining. Let this dry for twenty-four hours. You will be able to sponge this out when it gets filled with crumbs. Do not run water in it, however.

Decide where your stenciled letters will go on the top before applying the designs (Fig. 4–29). If you save a few cutouts you can arrange them around the word "cookies" or whatever you've chosen to use. Sheets of cutout stencil letters are inexpensive and sold in five-and-ten-cent, variety and stationery stores.

Using a pencil, first stencil out the word on a scrap piece of paper. You will then use this as a guide. Stencil the outline of the word onto the cannister with a

Fig. 4–28 Once lined the inside can be varnished two or three times to protect it.

Fig. 4–29 Stenciled letters are created for the word on the top.

Fig. 4–30 Once penciled on, each letter is carefully painted using a narrow sable brush. These letters are pink.

Fig. 4–31 More designs are added to the top and around the front catch before varnishing.

pencil. The color for this must be light enough to show up on the black paint. This one is pink. With a fine-pointed artist's paintbrush, carefully fill in the outlined letters (Fig. 4–30). Let this dry before placing the cutouts around it. Once the top has been completely designed and the excess glue has been removed from around the cutouts, it can be varnished. Apply several coats of varnish until you have created a smooth surface. Each coat must dry before applying the next. If the designs are slightly raised, this will add interest (Fig. 4–31). This is achieved by the number of coats of varnish used. The more varnish, the more your design will be submerged. If you only apply three or four coats, the design will feel slightly raised when you touch the surface.

Use a clean rag to apply a thin coat of clear furniture paste wax over the outside of the cannister. When buffed, this will protect the finish and give your piece a glow.

5

Decoupage On Glass

Decoupage can be done as successfully on glass as on any other surface. The process is exactly the same as on wood or metal, only in reverse. That is, the glue is applied to the front of the picture and the design is secured on the inside of the jar. The painting is done last, rather than first. So, once the picture is glued to the glass from the underside, it is coated with paint. In other words, the design is now under glass and the painted surface is inside the glass object. This paint is then protected with varnish. The background color is quite important because it will not be covered with varnish which usually gives the flat painted surface a little shine. In this case there will simply be a flat background color.

There are all kinds of projects that can be done using this process. Glass cannisters, apothecary jars of every size, glass plates, ashtrays, mason jars and plant holders are just a few of the things that can be made to look quite elegant. Many glass objects are sold in well-stocked craft shops, but the best place to look is probably a hardware store. If there is a pottery store in your area, you can find a large variety of things to choose from. You might like to practice on an inexpensive glass plate or ashtray before doing a larger project. Glass hurricane lamps have become quite popular for decoupage. If your craft shops don't carry them, ask them for a source. Sometimes hardware or department stores carry them.

Some craft shops have special glue for doing decoupage on glass, but Elmer's Glue All diluted slightly with water will work just as well.

83

APOTHECARY JAR

Materials Needed

apothecary jar (any size)   polyfoam brush or small sponge
paper designs   white glue
scissors   paint
polymer medium

Directions

This project is not difficult at all. Apothecary jars are fine for decoupage. This jar came with a paper wrap insert with colorful pictures of suggestions for things to put in it (Fig. 5–1). This sheet pictured green asparagus, brown cigars,

Fig. 5–1 A glass apothecary jar can be successfully decoupaged.

blue pencils and red and white peppermint sticks. This is used for the design element. Each picture is first cut out (Fig. 5–2). Next the designs must be placed inside to see how they will fit and if they need trimming.

These pictures are quite common. However, any design that is printed on lightweight paper will do. If you choose a greeting card, it should first be peeled in order to thin out the paper. Start with an edge of the card. Lift a corner of the back of the paper with the tip of your scissors and peel away a layer of paper. It is really best to find designs that are the right thinness. Wrapping paper or book pages are quite good. Magazine paper is too thin and the print will show through

Fig. 5–2 This design came right inside the jar. It is very colorful and easy to cut out.

from the underside when glued in place. Do not use magazine pictures for decoupage on glass.

Once the design is cut out, it can be glued in the following way. Place the design face up on a table. Squirt some glue onto the face of the design (Fig. 5–3). You might want to thin the glue slightly with water so that it won't be too thick. If it is not thinned it will work, but the next step will take a bit longer. With your finger spread the glue out evenly over the design. Lift it carefully and place it inside the jar so that the design is facing out. Place your hand inside the jar and begin applying pressure to the back of the design. Looking through the jar from the front, you will see the white glue on the design. As you apply pressure with your fingertips you will see the glue thin out and become clearer (Fig. 5–4). Apply pressure from the center of the design, moving to the outer edges. This will force out the excess glue which will then be wiped away with a wet sponge. Continue to do this until the design is securely fixed to the glass surface and all glue is forced to the edges.

If you have cut out very delicate designs, or if you are working on a hurricane lamp, it will take some extra care. Once you have decided where each design element will be placed, you can make a mark with a grease pencil on the glass. The grease pencil can be purchased in a photographic supply store or an art

Fig. 5–3 When doing decoupage under glass, the glue is applied to the front of the design.

Fig. 5–4 Press the design up against the glass, forcing the glue out the sides by smoothing it firmly with your fingers.

or stationery store. Hold the design inside the glass and with the other hand make an outline on the outside of the glass using the grease pencil. Then when you remove the design, you will have an indication for placing it exactly where you want it. Once the designs have been glued into their proper places, the grease pencil marks can easily be removed with a clean cloth.

After the designs are glued to the glass, the underside is painted. First, be sure that all edges are completely glued all around. If there is a raised edge that has been missed, the paint will seep under and ruin the face of the design. Since you want to avoid paint streaks or brush marks, the paint is patted on with a sponge or polyfoam brush (Fig. 5–5). Choose a color that will be pleasing against

Fig. 5–5 Using a sponge brush, the paint is applied to the inside of the jar.

the designs that you've placed on the glass. The acrylic paint is very good for this sort of project. When paint is too thin, it does not cover well. It is a bit more difficult to paint glass than wood, for instance. It will also take longer to dry. The acrylic paint is the right consistency and should not be thinned. Mix enough paint to cover the entire surface. If you are not mixing colors, you can squirt what you need from the tube onto a scrap piece of paper as you use it.

Do not brush the paint onto the glass. Pat it on. Keep patting until the glass is completely covered. This first application will not be a solid coating when viewed from the front. However, once the paint is completely dry you will apply another coat of paint in exactly the same way. If you find that a third coat of paint is needed, be sure that the second coat is dry before applying another. After the second or third coat, the glass will be completely covered. The color used here is beige.

Once the paint is sufficiently coated over the inside surface, it is protected with varnish. For this, the fast-drying polymer medium is best. You can use the same polyfoam brush after it has been cleaned well in water. It doesn't matter whether the finish is matte or glossy since it will not show. This coating is simply to protect the paint from chipping and so that you can put food into the jar if desired. Two coats of the varnish should be sufficient. This will take ten minutes to dry.

If you would like to see the objects inside the jar, it is not necessary to paint the inside. After the designs have been glued to the inside, several coats of the polymer medium can be brushed over the underside of the design. This should not be patted because it will create a foam which will dry in white bubbles. If the polymer medium is used, it should be brushed out so that it goes on in a thin coating. It will look white and murky, but will dry so that it is clear. Decide whether you want a matte or glossy finish if you are using the varnish without a painted background. In this case the finish will show up.

GLASS COASTERS

Materials Needed

glass coasters   felt material
cut-out wildflowers (paper)   glue
paint   scissors

Directions

The glass coasters are done exactly the way the apothecary jar was done except each is painted with a different color background (Fig. 5–6). The wildflowers are cut from a book of flowers and the colors correspond to the flowers. Once the paint has dried, each coaster is placed on a felt circle. Using a regular felt material, lay the coaster down and draw a circle around it. Spread glue on the bottom of the coaster. Do this sparingly. Place the cutout circle of felt on top of the glue and press it down. If there is any excess felt around the edge, it can be trimmed with cuticle scissors. This felt will protect the tabletop when a glass is on the coaster.

Fig. 5–6 Small round glass coasters can be designed with different flowers cut from a paperback flower book. Designed by Ruth Linsley.

6

Decoupage On Plastic

Decoupage is a little bit tricky on plastic because there are many different types of plastic and some surfaces work better than others. If the plastic object is to be painted first, note that some surfaces take the paint better than others. For instance, the plastic egg containers from L'Eggs stockings look best when painted with nail polish. A thin, water-base paint such as latex often pulls away from the plastic surface. Because some plastic is quite flexible, the varnish is not enough to hold the design in place forever.

There are, however, excellent plastic objects that are very good for decoupage. The heavy plastic plant pots, for instance, are very good (Fig. 6–1). Buttons can be designed with small cutouts and when sewn on a child's sweater can make it quite unique. Necklaces, earrings and bracelets, such as wide bangles, are great for decoupage designs. Since these objects are quite inexpensive, it is certainly worth exploring the possibilities. Plastic that is clear should be treated much the same way as a glass object. For opaque objects, the designs are applied to the surface as with wood or metal.

There is absolutely no preparation needed for this project. The surface of a Lucite plant holder is smooth and needs no sanding. Here is an opportunity to find a delicate design that will look well on this particular object. Remember that when it is filled the color of the dirt will be your background. This project was planned to hold a cactus in sand. Since the color of sand is light beige, the designs were chosen because the butterflies are dark brown and burnt orange. The blades of grass are moss green. If you will have dark earth in your pot, then your designs should be light and bright.

Fig. 6–1 A subtle design can be created on Lucite.

LUCITE FLOWERPOT

Materials Needed

clear Lucite flowerpot
polymer medium (glossy)
polyfoam brush

dark colored butterfly designs
scissors

Directions

The polymer medium glossy can be used as glue and varnish for this project (Fig. 6–2). It adheres well to the Lucite and dries with a clear finish.

First cut out the designs that you will be using. If the blades of grass are too long for the item, they can be shortened. Cut apart a solid design in order to fill out more of the space. Use cuticle scissors for cutting and be sure to eliminate any excess white paper, not only around the design but between grasses and leaves as well. A choppy cutting job will show up quite prominently on this project, so it is important to take time to do this well. Since the overall steps take so little time, it is well worth your while to spend a little extra time cutting out the design as perfectly as possible.

Apply the polymer medium to the inside of one section of the planter. Immediately press the design against the inside surface where the varnish has just

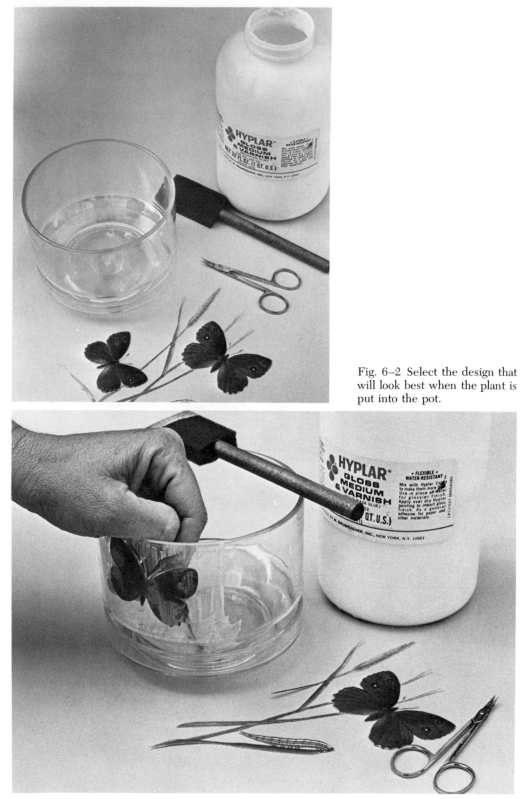

Fig. 6–2 Select the design that will look best when the plant is put into the pot.

Fig. 6–3 The clear water varnish is applied to the inside of the pot. The cutout butterfly is then pressed, face out, on the varnish.

Fig. 6–4 The back of the design is then protected with a coating of clear varnish. This will look murky when wet, but dry clear.

Fig. 6–5 The dandelions are glued to the front of this plastic flowerpot and covered with a clear matte varnish.

93

been applied (Fig. 6–3). Press it firmly all over. The whiteness of the varnish will disappear as it dries. Apply more varnish to the next area to be covered with a design. Do this until the area has been sufficiently covered. Apply a coat of the varnish over the back of the designs and continue the coating on the rest of the inside surface (Fig. 6–4). In this way the whole piece will have the same look. Brush the varnish on as smoothly as possible. A thin coat is better than a thick one. Since it dries so quickly, you can reapply the varnish every five minutes. Five or more coats are necessary to protect the design. Apply the varnish to the inside bottom as well so that when the plant is watered the water won't seep up under the designs. And that is all there is to it.

A Lucite cutting board or hot plate can be treated the same way. If you apply a design to the underside of a clear board, the design will appear to be imbedded in the plastic. For this you might want to paint the underside or leave it clear so that the table surface shows through as the background.

The dandelion design on the Christmas Cactus plant is glued to the outside of the pot as on any other surface (Fig. 6–5). The difference is that the pot wasn't painted first. The design was simply glued on and varnished over. This time a matte varnish is used, creating more of an opaque finish. Several coats of varnish are applied over the design. Since the varnish covers the surface of the dandelions several times, it is not as clear as the butterfly decoupaged pot. Either way, decoupage is successfully used on this surface.

MULTICOLORED EGGS

Materials Needed

L'Eggs egg (stocking package)   brush
several different colored tissue papers   razor blade
polymer medium

Directions

By now the plastic package shaped like an egg and used to hold stockings has been used for almost everything. It has been decorated with material, beads and cutout paper designs; it's been painted and hung from a Christmas tree. If you would like to experiment with different kinds of designs, these eggs are quite inexpensive considering that you are getting a pair of stockings in the bargain. Some variety stores sell packages of the plastic eggs that are slightly smaller than the L'Eggs eggs. They come in different bright colors and are most popular at Easter time.

To decoupage the eggs with different cutouts can be an interesting way to make Christmas ornaments. Use Christmas wrapping paper for the designs. You can buy the eggs in shimmery gold or silver for a seasonal touch. Heat a regular embroidery needle and push it through the top in order to make a hole for easy hanging. Loop a piece of gold wrapping string and tie a knot inside the top of the egg. Hang the egg over a branch on your tree.

If you'd like to give some candy as a gift you might decorate the egg with

Fig. 6–6 Plastic eggs can be decoupaged in many ways. Tissue paper in a variety of colors is used here.

colored tissue paper (Fig. 6–6). Or, if you are giving a piece of jewelry for a gift, you could line the inside with a pretty soft fabric.

The polymer medium acts as an excellent gluing agent and works best when the paper is thin. The tissue paper is an excellent weight for this. Stationery stores usually carry a selection of brightly colored packages of tissue. Buy the brightest you can find. If you can't find this in a stationery store, an art supply or craft store might carry it. Card shops often stock bright tissue paper.

Begin by tearing different shapes and sizes in each color (Fig. 6–7). They should not be too big. Keep the egg closed while working on it. Coat a section of the egg with the polymer medium. Decide before you start whether you'd like a glossy or matte finish. As you coat the varnish on the egg, lay a piece of tissue on the egg. Keep brushing the varnish onto the surface and placing more tissue on the egg. Overlap some of the pieces. Almost any pattern that you create will look good. When overlapped, the colors will change. The combination of the pastel colors will create another color in that section. Continue doing this until the entire egg is covered and there is no part of the egg showing.

Next brush a coat of the polymer medium all over the egg and tissue design (Fig. 6–8). Let this dry. Apply another coat. If you apply several coats of varnish, eventually the tissue pieces will be completely submerged. Since the paper is so thin this will not take too many coats. Let the whole thing dry completely. Using a razor blade, slice through the paper and varnish all the way around where the top and bottom come together. Pull the two halves apart. You can continue the process on the inside or you might like to line it with another paper. The paper lining will have wrinkles in it. However, the thinner the paper, the easier it is to

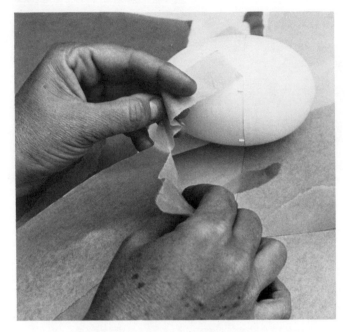

Fig. 6–7 Rip strips of tissue paper to apply to the egg.

Fig. 6–8 Use the polymer medium varnish as a glue to hold the thin tissue strips. Apply three coats of the varnish over the finished design.

smooth them out when varnishing. Or you can paint the inside with a brightly colored nail polish. Acrylic paint will adhere to the plastic, but not as well as nail polish which is also a lot less expensive. The nail polish will also dry faster than the paint.

Make several of these eggs and hang them on a branch for an Easter egg tree. This is an easy and quick decoupage project for creating a package that will not be thrown out once the gift is opened.

7

Decoupage On Soap and Wax

When doing a decoupage project on soap or wax, it is done a bit differently than the other projects. As with all decoupage projects, there is always cutting involved at some point. However, even the idea of decoupage being purely the art of cutting has been stretched a bit. Pressed flowers have been cut apart to apply to the candle while the paper cutouts are reserved for the soap.

The different element here is the finish. While we have been using different kinds of varnish, it cannot be used for coating a piece of soap or a candle. Each of these projects is coated with melted paraffin. Paraffin is clear wax and comes in a solid cube. This can be inexpensively purchased in a box at a hardware store or sometimes the supermarket. It is very easy to use. The paraffin is first melted on the stove, then the object is dipped into the hot wax and when cool dries to a clear hard surface. Of course, it is not a hard surface like varnish but the wax coating protects the decoupage, making the object useable.

Now you might think that decoupaged soap is going a little bit too far, but it really does work and the paraffin surface doesn't wear away. The underside of the soap is what is used. As for the candle, the best kind to use is that which burns down from the center, leaving the sides intact. They are generally dripless.

Sweet Heart soap is the perfect size and shape for this project (Fig. 7–1). It also has a design in relief on the top which adds a decorative touch when painted with gold. This accentuates the design giving it a border. Save greeting cards that have flower bouquets on them. These are the perfect thing for decorating soap. Once again, wrapping paper is also quite good. The paper is thinner than that of the cards and is therefore easier to cut out and will adhere well to the soap's surface. Old-fashioned valentine theme paper is used on the project here.

97

Fig. 7–1 Decoupaged Sweet Heart soap pieces designed by Anna Zuckerman.

SWEET HEART SACHET

Materials Needed

Sweet Heart soap   pair of tongs
flower designs to cut out (greeting card)   small, pointed paintbrush
paraffin   gold paint
small pan   scissors

Directions

First cut out some of the flowers that will be arranged on the soap (Fig. 7–2). Because the area to be covered is quite limited, there is not much cutting to be done. An overall design will look best. Avoid tiny delicate vines and buds. Try to avoid very pale pastel colors; the colors should be bright. Once the paraffin is coated over the design, it will dull it slightly. The design will look best if it overlaps. Leaving lots of empty space is not as desirable because the idea is to cover the top with a design. This is not treated as a three-dimensional item, such as a box. You are working with one surface, just the top.

Once the design is planned, put the cutouts aside. Using an artist's finely pointed brush, you will outline the soap. Gold leaf that comes in a small bottle at a craft shop can be used. Acrylic paint can also be found in gold metallic. Care-

Fig. 7–2 Wrapping paper, greeting cards or books provide a variety of flowers for this project.

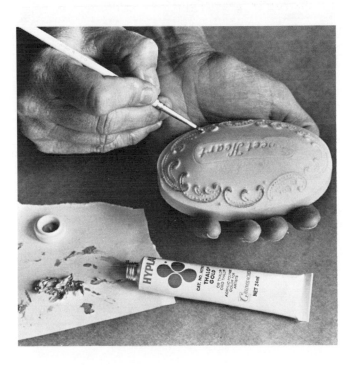

Fig. 7–3 The border can be outlined with gold paint before the designs are applied.

fully paint over all the raised areas, forming the design around the soap (Fig. 7–3). Only Sweet Heart soap has this delightful touch. Let the paint dry. It takes minutes.

Place a cube of the paraffin into an aluminum pan on the stove. It will melt

Fig. 7–4 The soap is dipped into hot melted paraffin before the paper cutouts are adhered.

very quickly. Once it has melted, turn the heat down to low so that it will not begin to harden while using it. If the surface begins to form a skin, raise the heat to melt it again. Hold the soap by its edges with a metal tong and dip it into the paraffin (Fig. 7–4). Do not dip it all the way in so that it is submerged. Simply touch the surface of the paraffin so that the top of the soap is coated. Remove the soap immediately. As quickly as possible place the cutouts onto the hot wax surface. Press the cutouts down so that they stick to the soap (Fig. 7–5).

Once again, pick up the soap with the tongs and dip the surface, with the designs on it, into the hot wax. Remove it at once so that you do not get too much of a build-up of wax. This will dull your design. Put the soap aside to dry and cool. This will take a couple of minutes. Once cool, the surface of the designs will be coated with wax and completely protected so that the soap can be used.

Fig. 7–5 Press the paper designs onto the hot surface.

PRESSED FLOWER SOAP

Materials Needed

Sweet Heart soap
fresh flowers
gold paint and small brush
tweezers

paraffin
small pan
pair of tongs

Directions

If you would like to make this project with real flowers, the basic process is the same. Outline the soap design with the gold paint. If you would like to try a color that will match one of the flowers, this would look well also. The flowers you use whould be pressed at least a week ahead of time. Violets look especially pretty and they are small enough to fit on the surface of the soap.

Use a tweezers to pick up each flower and leaf. Dip the flower element into the hot wax and lay it in place on top of the soap (Fig. 7–6). Be sure that the wax is very hot so that it will allow the flower to adhere to the surface. The hotter the wax, the less dulling the effect. Continue to add leaves and flowers to the overall design pattern. Press each in place with your fingertip (Fig. 7–7).

When all the flowers are in place, lift the soap with the tongs and dip the top surface back into the hot wax. This will coat and protect the pressed flower design. The soap is then ready to use.

This is a wonderful idea for the bathroom if company is coming. It makes a delightful gift when placed in a package with lingerie, for instance. You might also make a few to put in drawers as sachets or in the linen closet to keep everything smelling sweet. It is a pleasant surprise to open a dresser drawer and find this pretty touch.

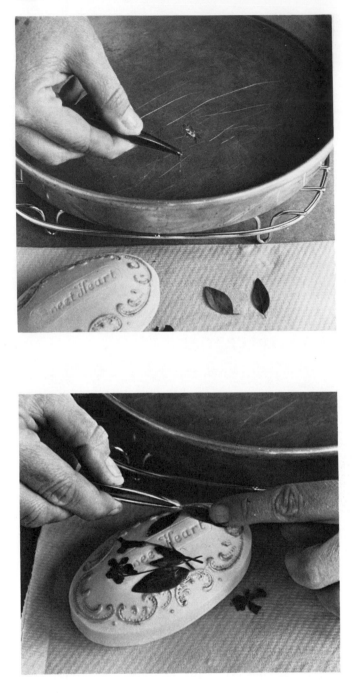

Fig. 7–6 Real pressed flowers are dipped into the wax before applying to the soap's surface.

Fig. 7–7 Hold the flowers with a tweezer to make it easier for placing.

It is very easy to make an unusual, personalized candle in minutes. Decorating a candle with real pressed flowers is a great way to change an ordinary candle into a really exquisite one (Fig. 7–8). Use it as a centerpiece for a table setting. The best type of candle for this project is the dripless, fat, white candle that is available in all candle and variety stores. When the candle is decoupaged with the real flowers, they seem to glow from behind when the candle is lit.

Fig. 7–8 An ordinary white candle made unique with pressed real flowers.

PRESSED FLOWER CANDLE

Materials Needed

5″–6″ tall, fat, white candle	pan
variety of pressed flowers	paper towel
cube of paraffin	

Directions

The first thing to do is to collect a variety of flowers. Of course, this depends on the time of year and where you live. When doing craft projects of any sort, it is a good idea to collect and press flowers when they are in bloom. They can be stored away for future use and it is an exciting discovery to find pressed marigolds or dogwoods in the middle of winter. The wildflowers are best for pressing and can be found in a variety of colors. Buttercups, violets, dandelions and Queen Anne's lace are but a few of the flowers easily found in the spring in most parts of the country.

It is very easy to press flowers. Check the previous project "Pressed Flower Decoupage" for directions. When out walking take along a few regular envelopes so that you can pick flowers and preserve them until you get home. You might like to keep each flower in a different envelope and press it this way. You can mark on the outside of each envelope the name of the flower contained within.

Place the envelope with the different flowers in between the pages of a very heavy book. Do not overlap flowers. The flowers that are the brightest colors are best for the candle project. Since the paraffin coating will dull the color a little, it is the vibrant colored flowers, such as violets, that show through better than others. However, if you would like to create a subtle effect, light flowers such as Queen Anne's lace can be quite effective. Once your flowers are pressed and ready to use, you can begin. If you have pressed enough flowers, you can do more than one candle at a time. This might be a good idea since the paraffin is messy even though the project is very easy.

Melt a cube of paraffin in a pan on the stove. Hold the candle at either end and roll the surface around to coat it with wax on one side (Fig. 7–9). The paraffin

Fig. 7–9 Roll the candle in hot, melted wax before applying the pressed flower designs.

should be very hot and this should be done quickly. Lift each flower and place it onto the waxed surface of the candle. If the paraffin cools while you are adding flowers, dip it quickly into the wax again. Keep adding flowers as you dip a section of the candle into the wax. You don't have to be overly concerned about the design since the wildflowers design themselves. The color, shape and texture of each flower is an interesting factor and almost any way that they are placed seems to look well. The dogwood on this candle is pink and white (Fig. 7–10). The very bright purple of the violet and green of the stem adds a nice touch to the more subtle colors of the dogwood (Fig. 7–11). The leaves were pressed in the fall and are a deep wine color.

When the flowers have all been pressed into place, hold the candle at each end and roll it around in the hot wax. Be sure that the candle is not submerged but just barely touching the surface. Remove and let the candle cool. Since the

Fig. 7–10 As each flower is applied, dip the candle once more in the wax to coat the designs and to heat the area to be designed next.

Fig. 7–11 Press the delicate flowers into the hot wax surface.

candle burns down through the center, the flowers will remain intact until the wick has burned down to the end. As the candle gets smaller inside, the light from within will make the flowers glow. It creates a very pretty effect.

If you are making this project for a gift, you might wrap it up with bright colored tissue paper, tie it with a ribbon at the top and add a few wildflowers.

8

Decoupage On Paper

Decoupage on paper might seem like decoupage on decoupage. However, a paper surface can be provided in many different forms. There are all kinds of paper and many objects are made of a paper that is as heavy and sturdy as any of the other surfaces used for decoupage (Fig. 8–1). Decoupage cutout designs have been used to decorate a plain paper plate which is then trimmed with lace and ribbon and hung as a decoration. A scene can be cut out and created on a heavy cardboard background or on colored poster board. The illustration can then be framed and hung.

Cardboard containers, such as the oatmeal boxes and similar objects can be used as cannisters or catchalls. Heavy paper paint buckets are perfect for decoupage and can be used to hold odds and ends or in a child's room as a toy collector. Decoupage can be applied to construction paper to create interesting original greeting cards. Before you throw away a cardboard box, like a tissue holder or a cigar box, think about using it for a decoupage project.

Tubes that hold toilet tissue or paper towels can be used. Cut them into several two-inch wide rings and paint them with acrylic paint. Cut out a different design for each, varnish them and use them for napkin rings. Even Styrofoam cups can be used as plant starters. Varnish and apply a cute design on each one. The fast-drying varnish makes a project like this easy and fun to do on a rainy afternoon.

When using inexpensive throw-away items that are not very durable, it is best to keep the project simple and quick. If you are doing a decoupage project for which you will be using a favorite design that takes some time to cut out, save it for a more lasting piece. A wooden box is something that you can keep forever and is worth the time and effort that you will put into the work. When choosing

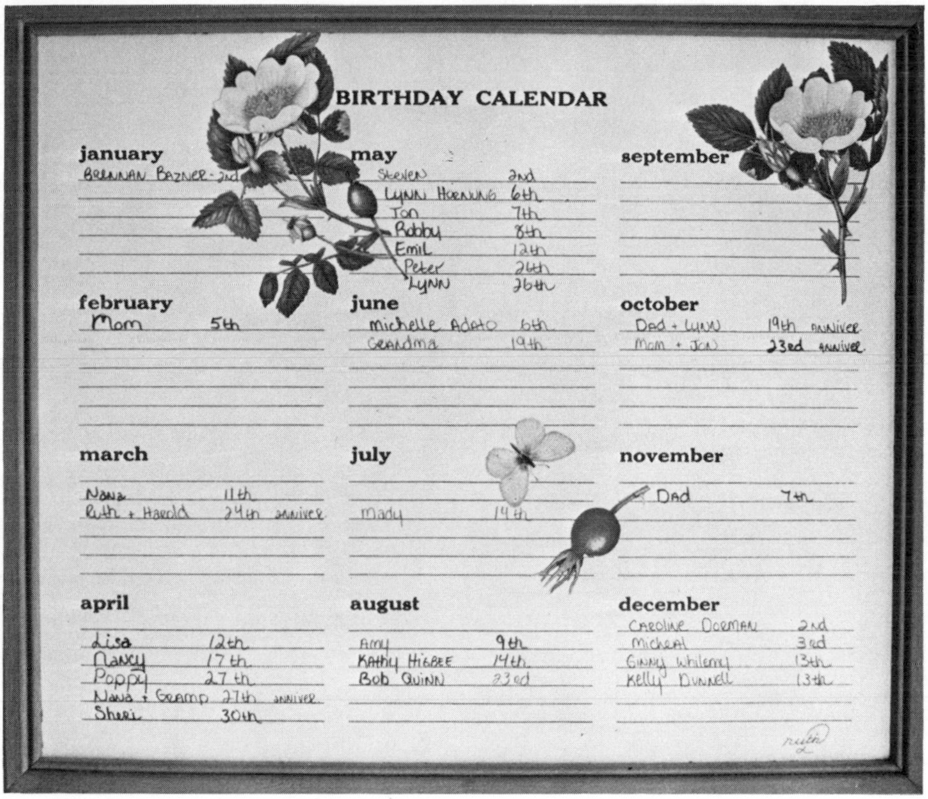

Fig. 8–1 Birthday calendar designed by Ruth Linsley.

the item and the design as well as the technique, evaluate the end results and the time you must put into the project.

Sometimes paper cutouts can be applied to a paper background and then secured to a wooden plaque or box in order to create a sturdier, more long-lasting project. The Birthday Calendar project was done this way although it could just as easily be framed without the use of the board.

Paper paint buckets are terrific for decoupage (Fig. 8–2). They come in different sizes and are available in any hardware store. They cost about 50¢ and can be used for a variety of things. Line them on a shelf in the kitchen to hold utensils. Or they could be used to hold yarn. Gaily colored and designed, they can be used in a child's room to hold toys. Make each one a different vibrant color. Paint the outside one color and the inside another. When choosing wrapping paper, pick designs that might look well when the buckets are sitting side by side. Perhaps the background color could be one color, while the same color is picked up in the design on another. The bucket here is painted with a bright orange-red (Fig. 8–3). No preparation is necessary. The buckets are made of heavy, white

Fig. 8–2 Inexpensive paint buckets make colorful catchalls.

paper and the surface is very smooth. The second bucket is left plain white, no painting necessary, and the inside is painted with the same bright orange-red of the first bucket.

CATCHALL BUCKETS

Materials Needed

paper paint bucket   glue
bright color acrylic paint   wrapping paper design
brush   varnish (glossy)
scissors

Directions

The wrapping paper selected for these two projects is bold and bright. The cutout designs are large flowers. One is an overall pattern of big bright yellow sunflowers (Fig. 8–4). The other is of bright orange-red poppies with brilliant green stems and leaves. Even though the designs overlap, you will be able to cut out sections to use. Cut the flower from one part if necessary, and cut the leaves and stem from another section. Piece and fit where necessary (Fig. 8–5). Cut out enough designs so that you can fill the area all the way around the bucket. It is easy to design these objects. The largest buckets allow more surface for design, but sometimes it is fun to combine the smaller and larger sizes.

Fig. 8–3 One coat of acrylic paint will cover the paper bucket sufficiently. Use bright colors for this project.

Fig. 8–4 Wrapping paper in bold designs is easy to cut and use to design this project. Use contrasting colors and cut enough to design around the entire area.

Fig. 8–5 Plan the design before gluing in place.

Once the designs have been cut out, plan where you will place them around the bucket. Apply glue to the back of each cutout and press it onto the surface (Fig. 8–6). Use a damp sponge to pat and pick up excess glue. Do not wipe across the design. Wrapping paper is often quite thin and can rip or wrinkle if rubbed.

Fig. 8–6 This bucket is painted only on the inside. The bright red poppies match the inside color. Here the stem is being pieced.

When the designs have all been glued in place, the entire bucket should be varnished inside and out. Use a glossy polymer medium varnish. This will give the piece a bright, shiny, sparkly look. Coat the bucket at least three times. Let dry five minutes between coats. This project is fun, can be completed in less than an hour and you can let your imagination run wild when designing.

For a different twist you might cut out letters that spell the name of something to apply and design around. Or the entire bucket could be covered with memorabilia or labels creating a collage effect.

A BIRTHDAY CALENDAR

Materials Needed

12″ × 14″ wooden plaque	flower prints
pastel acrylic paint	glue
brush	birthday calendar (see supply section)
sandpaper #320	sponge
scissors	inexpensive frame

Directions

A birthday calendar is an unusual project for decoupage (Fig. 8–7). Although the decoupage is done on a wooden plaque, this project can be put in an inexpen-

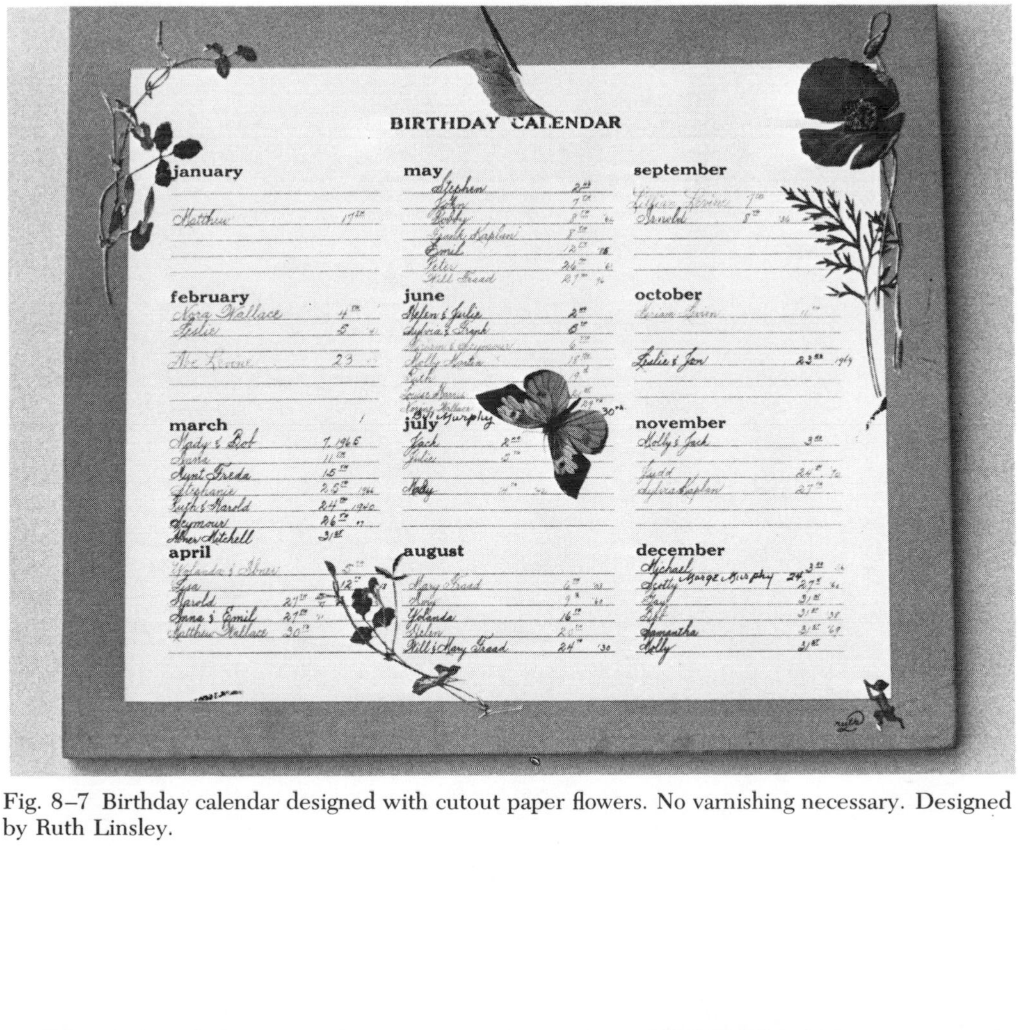

Fig. 8–7 Birthday calendar designed with cutout paper flowers. No varnishing necessary. Designed by Ruth Linsley.

sive frame which can then be painted to match the design. This is an original idea and the birthday sheet can be obtained through the mail. It is an excellent reminder of birthdays and anniversaries as well as an interesting wall hanging.

Begin by sanding the plaque (Fig. 8–8). This is a pine plaque available in any craft shop. Sand all the edges as they will be exposed. Next paint the plaque (Fig. 8–9). A light pastel color is usually a good background for this because the

Fig. 8–8 Sand a wooden plaque before painting.

Fig. 8–9 Paint around the outside and the rim where the board will be exposed.

flowers that you use for the decoupage will have a delicate feeling. However, if you will not be using flowers and have a bolder theme in mind, the background color is up to you. Since the birthday sheet will be glued to the board, it is not necessary to paint the entire surface. Paint around the front surface of the plaque so that when the paper is placed on top of it, there will be no area showing that has not been painted. Paint the edges. When this is dry, it should be sanded until smooth. If another coat of paint is needed, it too must be sanded when dry. Since this is the border outlining the birthday calendar, it is important to paint it well.

Apply white glue, such as Elmer's, all over the back of the birthday sheet. Wet a sponge to use for spreading the glue evenly over the back of the paper. The wet sponge will thin the glue enough for easy spreading.

Line the calendar up so that it is centered on the plaque (Fig. 8–10). Care-

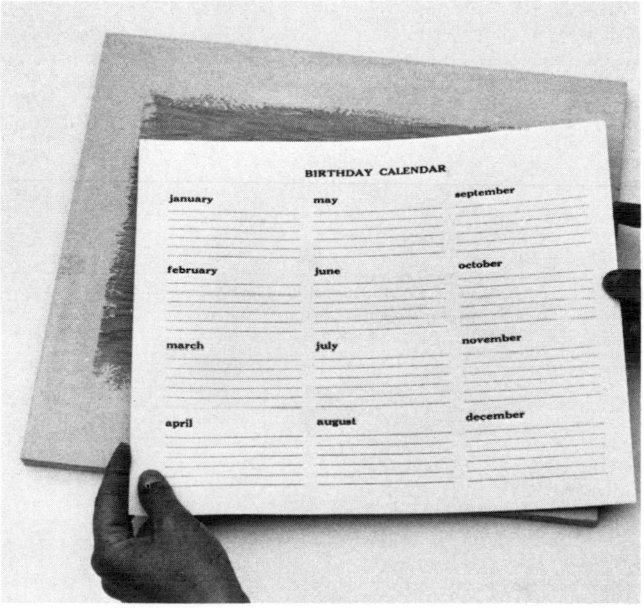

Fig. 8–10 Spread glue on the back of the paper calendar and center it on the plaque.

fully lay it in place and smooth it down with your hand. If you have a brayer, use it to roll over the entire surface. If not, a rolling pin or water glass will work well. This will eliminate bubbles and secure your paper to the board. Wipe around the edges with the sponge.

Choose flower prints that go together. You will need a few long-stemmed flowers to place on the sides (Fig. 8–11). A few smaller clusters will look well in between the months on the calendar sheet. Perhaps you can find a butterfly or two for added interest (Fig. 8–12). Blades of grass are always nice because they are delicate and will not interfere with the spaces for writing. Use heavier designs on the outside edges. This does not mean heavier weight paper, but rather larger, heavier-looking flowers. Design the flowers so that they overlap from the plaque onto the edge of the calendar sheet. The thickness of the cutout is unim-

Fig. 8–11 Design the flowers so that they look well on the plaque.

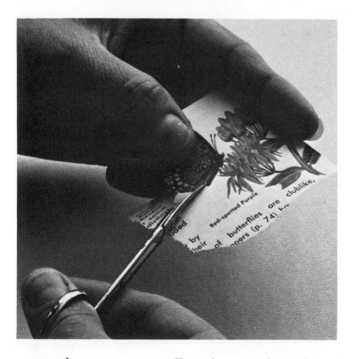

Fig. 8–12 Use cuticle scissors to cut the delicate designs for this project.

portant here since you will not be varnishing this project. You may decide to varnish around the outside, but it isn't really necessary.

Once all the cutouts are glued in place, you can fill in names of friends and family under the months of their birthdays (Fig. 8–13). Use a colored Magic

Fig. 8–13 Fill in names and dates, using a brightly colored Magic Marker.

Marker with a fine point. Choose a color that will look well with the color scheme of the flowers and background paint.

If you don't do this project on a plaque, it can be framed. Purchase the right size frame for the calendar. Take out the cardboard backing and lay the calendar on this while you are working on it. Cut out the designs as before and glue them in place here and there. Write the names and birth dates on the calendar and put the whole thing back into the frame.

Usually these inexpensive frames come with a black or natural color frame. Lightly sand over it to remove any wax. Mix the color of your choice using acrylic paints. Carefully paint the frame to match your design. If you are concerned about getting paint on the glass, you can place masking tape around the outer edge of the glass. Be sure that it is placed so that it is right up against the frame. When you paint, you can be less careful because the excess paint will simply be on the masking tape. When you are finished, pull up the masking tape and you will have a perfect paint job. If you don't mask the glass, wipe away any paint drips with a clean cloth as you work. If paint gets onto the glass and dries, it can easily be removed with a razor blade. If you want to protect the painted frame from chipping, you might varnish over the paint once it is dry. Do this only if you already have the varnish from another project.

The wooden plaque can be hung by a brass screw ring in the top or from the

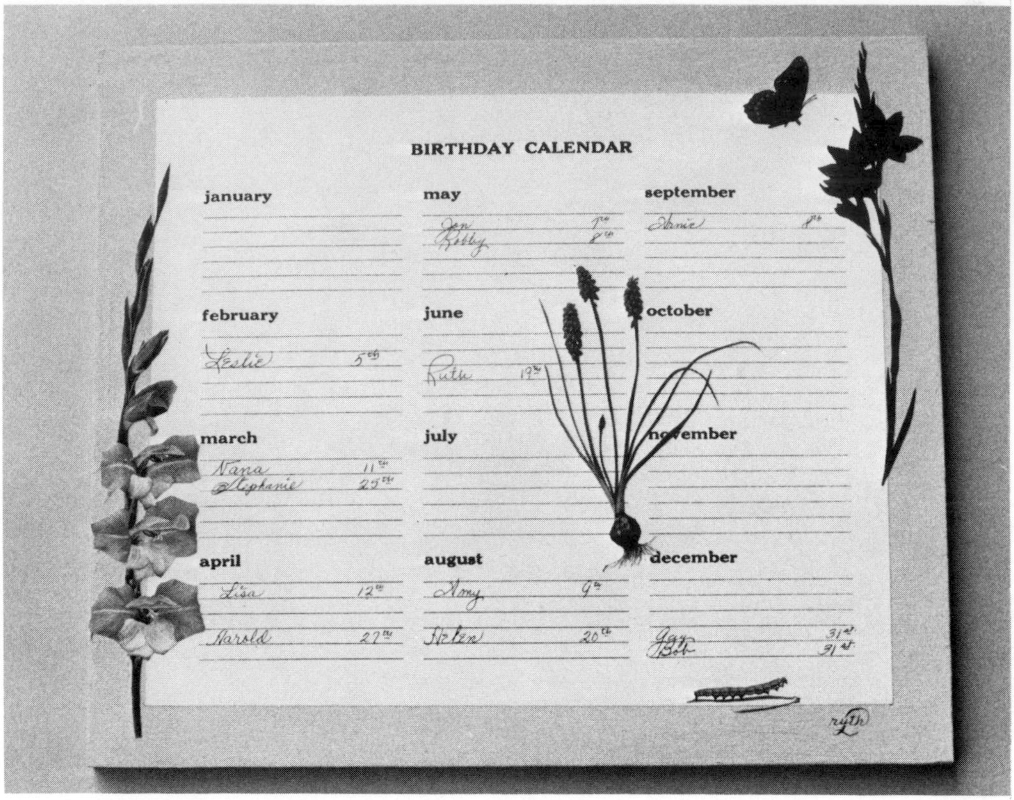

Fig. 8–14 Finished birthday calendar can be hung with self-adhesive picture hanger.

back with pressure sensitive picture hangers (Fig. 8–14). These are available in hardware stores.

There are several different ways to design this project. Look at some of the variations pictured here for ideas. Decide where you will hang it. This may determine the design.

SNAX STUFFERS

Materials Needed

oatmeal boxes (or similar box)	brush
wrapping paper	pencil and ruler
varnish	scissors
glue	label and letters

Directions

Cylindrical oatmeal boxes are terrific for cannisters, holding snacks and as catchalls for odds and ends (Fig. 8–15). Even buying a few will cost practically nothing. And if you don't like oatmeal, pour it all into a large coffee can and give it to a friend. As a matter of fact, you can use the large coffee cans with the plastic

Fig. 8–15 These snack stuffers are made from oatmeal containers.

lids for this project, but they do not turn out as well. For one thing, the can is not smooth; there are those ridges. Also they are not as nice a size as the oatmeal box.

Open the container and peel off as much of the label as possible (Fig. 8–16). The whole thing doesn't have to be clean but peel enough to eliminate any ragged edges.

Designs for this project can be fun. Choose wrapping paper for each one. This one is done with bright yellow and white daisies. If you make one to hold ribbons, you can use ribbon paper.

Place the empty cardboard container in the center of one edge of the paper. Roll the box and make a mark where the paper will be cut so that it fits all the way around the box (Fig. 8–17). Mark a line and cut. The varnish is not strong enough to use as the glue for this project. Squirt some white glue into a cup. Add a drop of water and mix. The glue should not be too thin, but it should be easily spreadable with a brush.

Brush the glue mixture over the entire surface of the oatmeal box (Fig. 8–18). Make sure that it is good and wet. Go over it again just to be sure—the wetter the better.

Place the glued container in the center edge of the paper. Press the edge of the paper against the box and smooth it down so that one end is secured to the box. With the other hand, pull the farthest edge so that it is taut. With the hand holding the box, roll it toward the outer edge smoothing the paper on the box as

Fig. 8–16 Before beginning, peel away as much of the wrapper as possible.

Fig. 8–17 Wrapping paper comes in a variety of patterns and colors. Choose a few that look well together.

you roll. It is difficult to keep the wrapping paper wrinkle free. Do this slowly and keep smoothing over the paper surface, pressing with your hand as much as possible. The wetter the box is, the smoother the paper will be because as it dries the paper will shrink onto the box.

Fig. 8–18 Apply glue to the box, not the paper.

Spread glue onto the bottom of the box and tuck the excess paper over the bottom (Fig. 8–19). With your brush add more glue to the bottom of the paper where it overlaps itself. Brush more glue around on the top of the inside of the box and tuck the excess paper on the top into the inside of the box. Press this down all the way around. Again, be sure that enough glue is applied.

To line the box, measure the length of the oatmeal box and cut another piece of wrapping paper. Spread glue over the inside of the oatmeal box. Make a roll of the paper so that the design is on the inside (Fig. 8–20). Insert this paper into the box. Press the paper to the outer walls of the box. Be sure that you work it around, smoothing it as you do this. Next, stand the box on a scrap piece of the

Fig. 8–19 Spread glue on the bottom and tuck the paper in.

Fig. 8–20 Line the inside with the same paper to complete this project.

paper and draw a circle around the bottom. Cut this piece out and glue it to the bottom.

Since the box is cardboard and has been quite wet with glue, it will have lost some of its stiffness. Let the whole thing dry for a few minutes. This will allow the paper a little time to adhere to the box.

While this is drying, you can cover the lid. Place the lid on a piece of the paper and draw a circle that is larger than the lid. It should be large enough so that there is enough paper to fold over and cover the inside rim. Brush the glue over the top and place it on the circle. Brush the outside and inside rim, making sure that it is very wet. Fold the paper up and over the rim, pressing it to the box as you turn it around. The paper on the inside will be folded as you go around. Keep applying glue as you work it around. Cut another circle the exact size as the lid and glue it to the bottom inside. Because the lid is not very sturdy when wet, it will be lopsided and out of shape. As it dries this will correct itself somewhat. Once varnished however, the stiffness will be returned and the top will fit perfectly.

Let the top dry. Rinse your brush out with hot water so that all the glue is removed from it before varnishing. The entire box can now be varnished inside and out. Before dipping the brush into the varnish, squeeze all excess water from it or this will thin the varnish too much. The varnish needs no thinning for this job. Brush the varnish on all exposed parts of the box; outside, inside, top and bottom (Fig. 8–21). The varnish will stiffen the container and give it a shiny finish. It will look highly lacquered and will be smooth to the touch. The more coats of varnish that are applied the better the container will look; and the sturdier it will be. Because the inside is coated, you will be able to store food inside without worrying about spoiling the container. No sanding is necessary between coats and since the varnish is fast drying you can apply five coats in less than a half hour.

Fig. 8–21 Several coats of glossy varnish will give this a shiny hard finish.

When the varnish has dried, you can make a label for the outside. This label comes in a package from the stationery store and is the kind that just adheres when the back is wet. Before applying it to the box, the letters are put on it. This can be done by writing them on with a Magic Marker or with cutout letters. You might want to stencil the letters. These were done with Press Type which comes in sheets from an art supply store, but this is an expensive way to get letters unless you will use them for other projects. One sheet of many letters costs about $4. Decide what your label will say, depending on what the container will hold, and apply the word. Stick the label in place on the container and apply a coat of varnish over it.

Make several of these containers and use one to bring some homemade cookies to a friend. Decoupaged packages confirm the fact that decoupage is definitely a recycling craft.

WILD CARDS

Materials Needed

construction paper   paper flower designs
scissors   pressed flowers
ruler   clear plastic Contact paper

Directions

A handmade greeting card can be a delightful way to cheer a friend (Fig. 8–22). It is much nicer than a card that you buy because it is like combining a little gift with your message. This project can be made on the spur of the moment

Fig. 8–22 A personalized card can be made in minutes.

if you find that you need a card or gift right away and haven't time to shop. Or you may make several at one time to have on hand for special occasions. And no two are ever alike.

These cards are designed on ordinary construction paper that is available in variety stores. It usually comes in a package and can be purchased in different colors. Be sure to decide what size you will make your card before buying your supplies so that you can get an envelope to fit.

One of the cards here is made with a cutout paper flower, the other is designed with pressed real flowers. If you will be using pressed flowers, begin by pressing flowers a week ahead of time. Check the other pressed flower projects for how to do this.

Fold a piece of construction paper in half one way. Next fold it in half the other way. Cut along the second fold line and the two halves will be your two cards.

Cut out a flower that will fit on the front of the card (Fig. 8–23). Or you might design the front with several flowers and butterfly cutouts. Perhaps you can find a flower to represent the birthday flower of the person who will receive the card. If you are designing the card with pressed flowers, arrange them on the card. These designs do not have to be glued in place. Simply lay them down where they look best (Fig. 8–24).

Fig. 8–23 Cut a paper flower to fit the folded paper card.

Fig. 8–24 Pressed flowers can be used for a different effect.

Cut a square of transparent Contact paper so that it is larger than the front of the card. This paper is available in hardware and dime stores. Peel away the paper backing and place the sticky transparent piece carefully on top of your design (Fig. 8–25). Once it is placed on the card, it cannot be removed so be sure that you place it correctly the first time. There should be an excess edge all the way around.

Fig. 8–25 Clear plastic paper covers the design. No varnishing at all.

Fig. 8–26 Trim the excess plastic and write your message inside.

Press the Contact paper down all over the front of the card. Smooth it out with the palm of your hand. Press it over all raised areas of the pressed flowers. The dogwoods used here were quite lumpy and needed firm pressure applied to make the Contact adhere to them. Using your scissors, trim around the paper, removing all excess Contact paper (Fig. 8–26). Open the card and write your message.

For this, choose a colored Magic Marker that will match the color of your flowers. This is a quick and thoughtful way to remember someone.

9

Decoupage On Ceramic

Some of the projects that can be done on ceramic are crocks that cheese comes in, cups, egg cups, even drinking mugs. Plant holders are beautiful when decoupaged. There is nothing special to know about doing a ceramic project except that the surface does not have to be painted. Most ceramic surfaces are smooth and have a glaze coating which is perfect for decoupage (Fig. 9–1).

Do not thin the glue when using it. It is easiest when thick because of the nonporous surface which makes it a bit more difficult to hold. You may find that on some ceramic surfaces, 3M Super Strength Glue is needed instead of the white glue.

CERAMIC CUP

Materials Needed

ceramic cup	sandpaper #600
glue	furniture paste wax
matte or satin finish indoor wood varnish	steel wool #0000
natural hair brush	black cutout silhouette designs

Directions

If the finish is white ceramic or porcelain, black silhouettes can be used for the decoupage design. This is what was used on the ceramic cup (Fig. 9–2). Simply spread white glue on the back of the silhouettes and press them in place on the cup. Be sure to roll your brush handle over each design to secure it firmly. Pat away excess glue with a damp sponge.

125

Fig. 9–1 A ceramic object does not need painting before applying the cutouts. Designed by Ruth Linsley.

When varnishing, keep in mind that the clear decoupage varnish has a slight yellow tint even though it is supposed to be clear. This is an advantage when applying to a stark white ceramic object. The many coats of varnish change the white color to a soft ivory, making the ceramic look like a piece of ivory. It is quite subtle and much nicer than the original bright white. The matte or satin finish indoor wood varnish is best for this even though it will take twenty-four hours between coats. Sand after the third coat of varnish so that you will not sand away any part of the design.

When applying the varnish, brush on a thin coat especially if working on a cup. If the brush is loaded with varnish, it will drip down the sides as it is drying. This is most undesirable and very hard to sand smooth once the varnish is dry. A thin coat will dry faster and you might be able to apply two coats in a day, one in the morning and one at night.

Hold your hand inside the cup while varnishing the outside. One coat on the bottom after you varnish the sides will seal the finish. Apply many coats of varnish so that when you feel the surface you can barely feel the design.

A natural hair brush should be used for varnishing and of course kept clean with brush cleaner, such as turpentine or mineral spirits. When you have finished varnishing, clean your brush, then rinse it out in hot water and soap. Wrap

Fig. 9–2 A black silhouette looks interesting against a white ceramic cup. Designed by Ruth Linsley.

in plastic wrap or a baggy and it will stay soft. A clean brush is the most important thing to ensure a beautiful finish.

Use the finest grade sandpaper, #600, for the final sanding. Dip this in sudsy water and sand over the piece. This will create a lather. Wipe this away with a sponge. Finally, rub steel wool #0000 over the surface. This will give you the finest, smoothest finish imaginable. Wipe away the steel wool particles and apply a thin coat of furniture paste wax. Butcher's Bowling Alley Wax or Johnson's is best. Let this dry for ten minutes. With a clean cloth rub and buff until a warm glow appears.

10

Decoupage On Rocks and Shells

Almost everyone has gone beachcombing when on vacation. Usually we collect shells and beach stones only to bring them home where they remain in a jar. Or they are thrown away after the vacation is over. A nice remembrance of a vacation is to make something with the natural found objects. Scallop and clam shells are probably the most common and provide a nice smooth surface for decoupage. The inside of shells has been naturally sanded by the waves and sand and just needs to be washed out before using. The decoupage can be applied right to the clean white shell or the shell can be painted. Try painting them metallic silver or gold for something unusual.

Jingle shells with tiny holes at the top are perfect for jewelry items such as a necklace or earrings. The tiniest decoupaged design inside each shell can be a pretty way to make more of a shell piece. Pick out seven or eight similar shells. String them on a silver elastic cord with a natural colored bead between each. In the center of each shell place a tiny flower. A ladybug or butterfly that is small enough to fit inside can be barely perceptible, like a found treasure. Or cut out a very decorative initial to place inside of one shell to wear on a chain. Attach a shell to a key ring holder and decoupage it with your favorite subject. The earring findings and the key rings and chains can be found in craft shops.

Rocks can be found everywhere. Big rocks, little stones, flat rocks and bumpy ones. Why would anyone want to decoupage a rock? There are some interesting things that you can do with a rock. A really huge rock can be used as a doorstop. A small rock can be decoupaged to use as a paperweight. Small stones are fun to decorate just to leave on a table or windowsill. Or you could actually make something out of the stones. Different shapes can be put together to form a miniature scene. A shape like a person could be decoupaged with cutout eyes, nose, mouth, etc. You can have a lot of fun making silly things with rocks.

Fig. 10-1 These rocks are designed with cards made into decals with Decal-It.

Since the surface of most rocks is not smooth, it is not easy to decoupage in the conventional way. Transfers or decals work best on rocks (Fig. 10-1). However, if you can find some really smooth stones, you will have a ready-made surface for some nice decoupage. Most common rocks, however, are not smooth. They are great looking when painted in bright colors. Acrylic paint covers a rock easily.

SHELL CANDY DISH

Materials Needed

scallop shell or large clam shell	scissors
brush	flower design
paint	glue
sandpaper #600	varnish

Directions

You can't beat the price of a shell for a decoupage project. Of course if you can't go to a seashore, you will have to buy one from a craft or shell shop. If there isn't one near by, you can order them through a mail-order house.

When looking for a shell to decoupage, look for one that is large enough to use. The smaller shells do not hold much. Find a shell that is smooth on the inside and free of cracks or imperfections.

Any craft paint will cover the inside of the shell (Fig. 10–2). The one shown in Fig. 10–4 is painted soft orange and the outside is left the natural shell color. The paint will take a little longer to dry than on wood or metal, but once dry will probably not need another coat.

Fig. 10–2 An ordinary clam shell can be painted for decoupage. It is already sanded by the waves and sand from the beach.

Select a design from a greeting card, a print from the craft shop or from a book. Be sure that it is small and in proportion to the shell. If the design is quite large, it will look overpowering inside the shell. The design should be delicate and appealing. If it is placed off to one side, you will be able to serve candy in the shell and the design will still show.

Use cuticle scissors to cut out the design. If you are using something very delicate, cut the petals and hard to get at places first (Fig. 10–3). If you hold your scissors so that they are pointed away from you, it will be easier to cut. If the scissors are turned in toward the design, you can make a mistake and accidentally cut off a petal or leaf. Cut the in-between places first so that you can hold onto the outside of the flower as you cut. Take your time cutting. Since you are not doing a large job, it is worth your while to take your time. This little flower is the only design, so make it perfect. Your scissors should be sharp at all times. This will make for a better cutting job. To keep them sharp, reserve them for cutting only. The more pointed and thin the blades are, the easier it will be to maneuver them into tiny areas.

Spread a little glue on the back of the cutout. Place the design on the painted surface where you have planned for it. With your fingertip, press down on the flower in every spot. Using the handle of the paint brush, tap it down on the flower. This will secure it to the shell. Since it is too difficult to roll the brush handle over the flower, this will force any excess glue out of the edges. Sponge it away lightly.

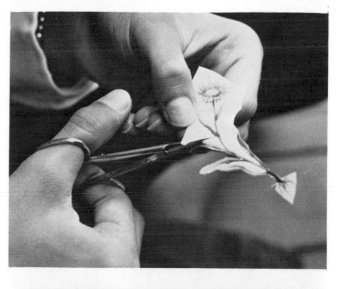

Fig. 10–3 Cut a small design that will fit inside the shell.

Fig. 10–4 This project can be displayed as is or used to hold candy or carefully used as an ashtray.

If you would like to have this project done quickly, use a polymer medium fast-drying varnish. The glossy finish is perfect for this project. If you would like a very smooth satiny finish, use the long-drying indoor wood varnish in a matte finish. Of course this will take longer to dry but the finish will be lovely. Five coats should be sufficient. Fill it with candy kisses and place on a table (Fig. 10–4). This can be a perfect project for a child to do.

LOVE STONES

Materials Needed

several smooth black stones
several small flower buds (paper)
scissors
glue
glossy varnish

small square of felt (color to match flowers)
brush
sandpaper #600
brush cleaner

Directions

Small stones can be made just to look pretty. They can be used for paper-weights or they can be sent in the mail to carry a message, like a card.

Find stones that are small and flat and smooth (Fig. 10–5). The black Japanese stones are best. Sometimes pottery stores or garden shops carry them. They are lovely and should not be painted before applying decoupage.

Fig. 10–5 Flat stones having a smooth surface can be decoupaged.

The small buds of flowers that are normally overlooked can be saved and used for the designs. Choose pale colors like pink or very light yellow. These will show up well against the black stones. When stones are wet, especially if they are black, they are shiny and bright. When dry the color is flat. The varnish will make the stones look as though they are wet and will keep them looking like they are underwater.

The cuticle scissors will enable you to cut the tiny delicate buds. Use good lighting so that you can see what you are cutting. This will be a challenge. Often these small designs are the parts that you cut away when doing larger projects. Sometimes they are so delicate that they cannot be seen on a page. However, once cut out and placed on a black background, they appear to be quite important. Perhaps this is due to the relation of the size to the stone. If the delicate buds are too difficult to handle, a tweezer is good for this.

Squirt a puddle of glue onto a scrap piece of paper. Pick up the cutout with the tweezers. Lay it gently across the glue and lift it onto the surface of the stone. Pat the design onto the stone with a slightly damp sponge. Press it down while lifting excess glue off the design and the stone. It is important that all glue is removed from the exposed surface. If some is left, it will cause a discoloration mark when the varnish is applied.

When all the stones have been designed, varnish each one. For this project use glossy decoupage varnish. The water-base polymer medium varnish is faster, but will not sand as smooth as the regular oil varnish. You may not feel that this project warrants a lot of time. However, the time is in the drying, not in the applying. Since the items are so tiny, you can run the varnish brush over all the stones in less than ten minutes. When dry, sand and continue to apply more coats of varnish. When the cutouts have been coated with enough varnish so that they are completely submerged, you will not be able to feel them. This creates an interesting effect. The surface is shiny and smooth and the design appears to be embedded in the stones.

Cut out a small round piece of felt for the bottom of each stone. Add a drop of glue to the bottom of each stone and apply the felt pieces.

If you'd like to try a more challenging project and a different use for the stones, try this idea. Purchase a wooden box in a craft shop. It should be a box with a removable top so that you can use only the bottom or the top separately.

Using the small stones, find letters that can be cut out to fit on them. The letters can be found in magazines and might spell something like "love is beautiful" or "be my valentine" or something more original that has meaning to you. The letters must fit on the stones so find words that are small enough to cut, but large enough to read easily. If they are to be used on black stones, the letters must be painted in a color that is bright enough to show up on the background. If it is possible to also find small designs that might work with the letters that will be great. Glue the letters on the stones so that one stone might have "lo" on it. The other might have "vei" with a tiny flower on it as well. The next, "sbe" and so on. Thus it will not be obvious what the stones say at a glance. The point is that the project, when finished, will be a simple puzzle. When the words have been spelled out on the stones, varnish each one several times.

Now, mix up enough plaster of Paris to fill either the top or the bottom of the box. The plaster of Paris is available in all hardware stores. The directions for the ratio of water and plaster are on the package. A small bag is all that is needed and it is quite inexpensive.

Put enough plaster into the box so that the surface is not smooth. It will stand in peaks and hold its shape so that you can play around with it. When the plaster is still wet, take each stone and make an indentation. Each stone should fit into a pattern so that when side by side you can read the saying. Perhaps you will have three rows of three stones each. The first three stones might read "lo", "vem", "ake", the next three, "sth", "ew", "orl", and the last three 'dgo", "rou", "nd".

Each stone should fit in its place. Each stone will have a different indentation in the plaster indicating its place. Once you have made an impression in the plaster remove the stone.

When the plaster has hardened, each stone will have its place where it will fit exactly. The stones are then put back into the plaster to create a decorative puzzle. If you would like to paint the plaster, this can be easily done with acrylic paint. By mixing metallic silver with any other color, you can create a colored metallic background. Pink mixed with silver makes a shimmery pink metallic. Paint the outside and rim of the wooden box in the color of your choice. If you want to make the plaster shiny, simply give it a coat of the glossy varnish when you are coating the stones. Of course it must be hard before applying the varnish.

ROCK STOP

Materials Needed

large rock   varnish (polymer medium glossy)
piece of felt large enough to fit bottom   Decal-It
paint   pan of water
brush

Directions

A large rock can be made to look quite novel as a decoupaged door stop. Or you might make two and use them as bookends. Since the surface is quite bumpy, it is almost impossible to apply decoupage to this surface in the conventional way. And since decals are limited in design, this isn't always a good way to design something. However, you can make your own decal and it can be any subject or picture that you want. Decal-It is a fairly new product available in craft shops. It is made to transfer a design from any card or similar design source onto any surface by turning it into a decal. This material lifts the picture right off its backing, creating a thin plastic film that stretches and then shrinks like skin onto the rock. It is also transparent, therefore, the background color shows right through the picture. When choosing the paint color keep this in mind. This material does not work well on magazine print. For best results greeting cards should be used.

Begin this project by looking for a really nice large rock. It should be as smooth as possible. Acrylic paint looks and covers well (Fig. 10–6). Choose a

Fig. 10–6 Begin by painting a few rocks, each in a different acrylic color.

pretty color that isn't too dark. Sky blue, pale pink and sunny yellow all look bright and pretty behind a picture.

Look for pictures that you find especially pleasing. Be sure that the cards you select will fit on the rock area. There is no cutting involved with this project; therefore, the picture will be used exactly as it appears on the card. This includes all the little details that might surround the main picture.

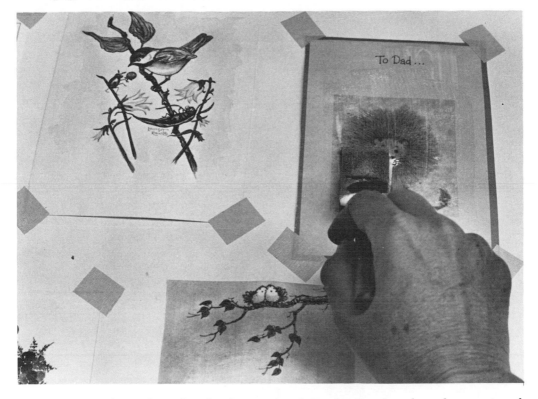

Fig. 10–7 Tape a few cards to a board and coat each with Decal-It. Let them dry and coat again and again.

Tape the pictures to a piece of waxed paper for easy handling. Using an inexpensive polyfoam brush apply the Decal-It over the picture and let it dry (Fig. 10–7).

Apply six coats of the Decal-It to the face of the print. Let each dry thoroughly between coats; set the pictures aside for two hours. After this, place the pictures in a pan of warm water and leave them there for an hour. Lift the pictures out of the water and lay them face down on the kitchen counter. Rub the paper backing off each picture. Use your fingers to do this (Fig. 10–8). Be careful not to rip the design or stretch the transfer. It should appear to be transparent when all the paper is removed from the back.

To apply the transfer or decal, apply a coat of polymer medium to the rock and lay the design in place (Fig. 10–9). Press it down with fingertips so that it adheres to the rock. Let this dry for a minute or two. The color of the paint will show right through the clear transfer.

Next apply two or three coats of varnish to the entire surface of the rock and over the design. This will give it a protective coating.

When the varnish has dried, place the rock on top of a piece of felt and draw around it. Cut this out so that it will not show when glued to the bottom portion of the rock. Since most rocks are uneven at best, the felt should only be where the rock will be resting on the floor or on a shelf. Apply white glue to the bottom

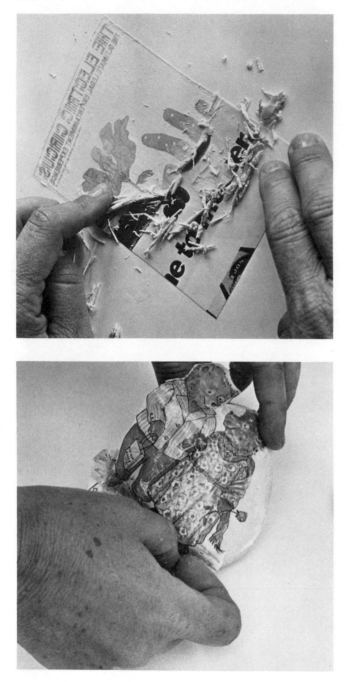

Fig. 10–8 Remove the back of the cards by soaking in water and rolling away the paper with your fingers.

Fig. 10–9 The picture will become a decal that is transparent and easily placed on the rock, using the polymer medium to hold it in place.

area to be covered. Lay the piece of felt on top of the glue and press down with the palm of your hand. Try not to apply too much glue so that you will not have it oozing out onto the felt. Turn the rock right side up. If some of the edges of the felt can be seen, trim this with your cuticle scissors.

Make a really large rock decoration and place it by your front door. Make lots of small rocks at one time to sell as fund raisers. Children can make them as school projects. Save old greeting cards to use for this.

11

Decoupage On Canvas

Decoupage on fabric? It will never work. A few years ago this might have been true; however, there are actually ways to glue paper to canvas with new fabric glue and it does work. If, for instance, you are applying cutout designs to a director's chair and want to extend the design over onto the canvas back it is possible. A drop of fabric glue made by the 3M company can be spread on the back of the paper design and it will hold to the canvas. Paintings of decoupage designs in relief can be arranged on a canvas background. By combining real flowers and paper flowers done in repoussé, you can create an interesting wall hanging for any room. This is an excellent way to make an original "painting" when you don't know how to draw or paint.

Artist's canvases come in many different sizes and are available in all art supply stores. Not only are the canvases available, but you can buy pre-scored, easy-to-fold canvas-like paper as well. This is less expensive and you might buy a couple in different sizes to try this craft idea. These paper canvases are made only by the Grumbacher Company. They even have holes pre-punched for easy hanging.

A tennis racket cover or a canvas carrying bag can be decoupaged with an interesting design that is one of a kind. The design will not be guaranteed to last forever because it is not advisable to apply varnish over it. However, a quick spray of Krylon will help and not hurt the canvas at all. This is a clear spray that is used to protect an artist's drawing done in charcoal or pastels so that they will not smudge.

Canvas espadrille shoes can be decorated with a small paper cutout design on each. Clogs, while not made of canvas, hold a paper cutout quite well. Dr. Scholl's sandals have been used quite often for decoupage. Apply a small delicate vine around the wooden part of the shoe.

REPOUSSÉ COLLAGE

Materials Needed

canvas 9″ x 12″
brush
paint (pale blue and white)
spray varnish
polymer medium
dried and pressed flowers

paper flowers
paper butterfly
real blades of grass and leaves
cuticle scissors
modeling paste

Directions

The natural collage is created by using a combination of flowers, grasses, leaves with paper butterflies and flowers which are glued to a painted canvas background (Fig. 11–1).

Fig. 11–1 A repoussé collage is shown here, using dried real flowers and leaves as well as paper grasses and butterflies.

The paper cutouts are made to look three dimensional by the use of repoussé. This combination of texture and dimension creates an interesting natural "painting."

To prepare for this project, press a variety of flowers and grasses that you will use. This is done by collecting different types of flowers and other natural materials during the seasons in which they are available. Start a week ahead of time. Choose flowers that are brightly colored and do not use a fat or pulpy blossom. These are most difficult to press. Every collage will be different, depending on the time of year that you do it and where you live in the country. If you visit another part of the country, it is always a good idea to pick the regional flowers to press. This is a wonderful reminder of your trip; and if you are a crafter, your collections will be invaluable. Best of all is the price. These can be the best souvenirs around.

Mix the blue and white acrylic paint to create a pale blue background. This is done by applying a dab of white on a piece of paper and adding a tiny amount of blue. If you want to invest in a palette pad, this is a pad of waxed paper made especially for mixing paints. After you use a sheet, you simply rip it off and throw it away. It is wax coated so that the paint won't soak through to the underside. Grumbacher makes this product and it is available in art supply stores.

Using your paintbrush, or even better a palette knife, mix the two paints together. Add a little more of the blue if you want it to be darker, or white if it should be lighter. The paint always looks lighter when on the paper in a small dab than when it is painted onto the canvas. When in doubt it is always best to go for the lighter shade. Everything will look better against a lighter color.

Apply the paint over the canvas. The painting need not be perfectly smooth as a textured look is desirable. Clean the brush in water so that there is no trace of the paint in the brush.

Once the paint has dried, plan your scene by temporarily placing the dried flowers, grasses, leaves on the canvas (Fig. 11–2). Move the elements around until you have created a pleasing arrangement. Plan the heavier ground cover for the bottom of the canvas. In that way you can place the blades of grass so that

Fig. 11–2 Plan out the scene before gluing in place.

they appear to be growing up from the bottom. When you place leaves across the bottom, they will cover the unevenness of the grasses.

Butterflies and flowers cut from paper can be found in craft shops or you can buy pre-cut seals. An inexpensive paperback book, such as The Golden Book series, has individual books of butterflies or flowers, animals or insects, as well as many other subjects. Use cuticle scissors to do the cutting. Select cutouts that are not too difficult and tiny. Flowers and butterflies with a good sized area to be raised are best for repoussé (Fig. 11–3). The designs that you cut from paper should design well with the natural elements of the collage.

Fig. 11–3 Cut paper objects that are large enough to use for repoussé.

Remove the natural pieces from the canvas, remembering where each will be placed when gluing. Brush the polymer medium over the canvas where each pressed flower will be placed. You may find that a pair of tweezers is helpful for lifting the dried flowers and blades of grass. Place each piece carefully on the canvas. The polymer will be clear when dry. This is easier to use than glue for delicate dried flowers.

Cover the bottom of stems with blades of grass or leaves set close together. Apply some polymer medium to the grass and place the dried leaves here and there on the bottom.

The raised effect is created by wetting and stretching the paper. The elevated process is called repoussé. To create this embossed effect with the paper cutouts, soak each piece in water. Using a spoon or similar rounded utensil, mold the wet paper cutout over it to dry (Fig. 11–4).

When thoroughly dry, turn it over so that the design is face down in the palm of your hand. Using a knife, scoop the modeling compound into the recessed cavity until it is almost level with the edges (Fig. 11–5). This compound is found in craft or art stores.

Fig. 11–4 Soak the butterfly cutouts and let each dry over the back of a spoon.

Fig. 11–5 Fill the cavity with modeling paste or similar material.

Turn the repoussé over and lay it in place on the canvas. Use the knife to press the edges down all around onto the canvas (Fig. 11–6). This design will be

Fig. 11–6 Set in place on the canvas and press the edges to the surface with a palette knife.

raised from the canvas surface, adding more interest than it would if simply applied as a flat cutout. This repoussé process can be used in many different ways. On a purse, you might have animal cutouts with parts of the body raised where it would be natural. Perhaps you have some paper mushrooms. This is an ideal subject for repoussé. Use a subject that would look natural with parts of it raised. The body of a bird, for instance, would look natural puffed out.

Once the entire scene is created and everything is glued in place, check to see if there are some awkward spots. Add leaves or grasses if necessary. Let this piece dry overnight so that the modeling compound can harden under the paper. When this dries, spray the entire collage with varnish medium (Fig. 11–7). This will protect the natural elements. Let this dry for several hours before hanging.

If you live in an area where there is a change of seasons, you could try four different collages. Change them on the wall, depending on the time of the year.

Fig. 11–7 Once the collage is dry, spray with varnish in order to preserve it.

12

Some Helpful Hints

By the time you have gotten to the end of the book, you will have tried decoupage on at least a few surfaces. Perhaps you have run into a problem or two along the way. Although the process is quite easy, there are a few things that are helpful in order to ensure good results. Some of these things are hard to anticipate before they happen.

What happens if you have paint drips that have already hardened on your piece? It is not unusual to think that they are unimportant and can be sanded smooth without much trouble. This is sometimes true, however, often not so easy. A razor blade comes in handy here. Slice the heavily dried area away, sand and repaint. Let's go on to a few other little problems that you may have encountered.

WARPING OF A BOX

If you find or have purchased a box that is slightly warped, don't go running back to the craft shop with it. This is easily fixed if the box is made of a soft wood like pine or birch. A warped box will not close properly. Fold a piece of shirt cardboard in half so that it is double thickness. Place it on the inside rim of the back of the box so that it butts up against the back hinge. Close the box a couple of times with the cardboard wedged inside. Do this with the cardboard against one hinge and then the other. Remove the cardboard and the box should close. If it doesn't, make the cardboard a little thicker and try again. This will loosen up the hinges and allow the tightness to disappear so that the box will close properly.

144

BUBBLES UNDER THE PRINT

If you have glued a print in place and it has dried on the surface of your project with an air bubble quite visible, this can be solved. Slice through the area with a razor blade and squirt some glue on the area. Work it under the design first on one side and then the other. This is not the best way to glue a design in place but if it means saving the print it must be done. If you have an air bubble under the transfer design, prick it with a pin and wet the area with the polymer medium. Press it back in place with your fingertip.

BUBBLES IN THE VARNISH

When applying the varnish to a surface, it often creates little bumps of air bubbles. If you hold the piece so that the light reflection allows you to see this, you eliminate the bubbles. When applying your oil varnish brush it across the piece in one direction. With the tip of your brush (a natural hair brush, not a polyfoam brush) pop the bubbles. Then bring the brush tip very lightly across the surface in the opposite direction from that which you did originally. Once dry, you will sand whatever dust away that has settled on the piece while drying. Checking the finish before it dries is always a good idea.

BRUSH BRISTLE DRIES IN FINISH

If, when you have finished painting or varnishing, you find that one of the brush bristles has dried in the finish, it can be removed. Using a razor blade, pick up one edge of the hair. Grab it by the end either with your fingers, if possible, or a tweezer and pull it up. Sand the area where the hair was removed. If there is a mark on the varnish, you can cover this up with a little antiquing. Of course, this means that the whole piece must be antiqued. If there are dirt particles that have dried on the piece, antiquing is a good cover up for this also.

NICKS AND BRUISES IN THE WOOD

If you have a box that has gouges or small nicks in the wood, this can be treated. Either sand and fill these areas in with wood putty which is available in a hardware store or sand and paint as usual. After the varnish has been applied plan to antique the box. The antiquing should be applied heavily in the bad areas. This will fill in, look quite natural and add interest to the piece.

PAINT ON THE HINGES

It is never necessary to remove the hinges from a box in order to paint it. Paint carefully around hinges and catches. If paint gets on the hinge and it has dried before you have had a chance to wipe it off, use a razor blade to remove it. Simply scrape excess paint off with the blade. Aside from this, the paint can be covered up with antiquing so the hinges look old and will match the rest of the box. This means that the whole box should be antiqued. If you aren't planning to antique, then be careful about the paint and try to do a real neat job. Some hinges are not good looking and you might want to cover them with paint intentionally. The stapled hinges are not that great and will work just as well if covered with paint. The part where the hinge bends, such as the inside, should be free of paint if possible. It is difficult to remove paint from inside this area.

Sources for Materials and Tools

All the craft materials used in this book are available in craft stores, hardware stores, discount department stores or through mail-order houses. If you have trouble finding supplies in the above places the following is a list of companies that carry decoupage supplies.

The O-P Craft Company
425 Warren St.
Sandusky, Ohio 44870

Connoisseur Studio, Inc.
Box 7187
Louisville, Kentucky 40207

Hazel Pearson Handicrafts
4128 Temple City Boulevard
Rosemead, Calif. 91770

For the Birthday Calendar
    send $2 to:
Birthday Calendar Inc., Box 102A
200 N.E. 20th St.
Boca Raton, Fla. 33431

Photo by Nancy Wayman

Leslie Linsley is a craft designer and the author of five other books, three of which are on decoupage. Her work appears regularly in the pages of national women's magazines, including *Glamour, House Beautiful, Good Housekeeping,* and *McCall's Needlework and Crafts.* She lives for part of the year in Westport, Connecticut, and the remainder on Nantucket Island, Massachusetts.